The New Rules of
INFLUENCE

The New Rules of
INFLUENCE

How to Authentically Build Trust, Drive Change, and Make an Impact

LIDA CITROËN

Berrett–Koehler Publishers, Inc.

Berrett-Koehler Publishers, Inc.
1333 Broadway, Suite P100
Oakland, CA 94612-1921
Tel: (510) 817-2277
Fax: (510) 817-2278
bkconnection.com

ORDERING INFORMATION
Quantity sales. Special discounts are available on quantity purchases by corporations, associations, and others. For details, contact the "Special Sales Department" at the Berrett-Koehler address above. For details, please go to bkconnection.com to see our bulk discounts or contact *bookorders@bkpub*.com for more information.

Individual sales. Berrett-Koehler publications are available through most bookstores. They can also be ordered directly from Berrett-Koehler: Tel: (800) 929-2929; Fax: (802) 864-7626; *bkconnection.com.*

Orders for college textbook / course adoption use. Please contact Berrett-Koehler: Tel: (800) 929-2929; Fax: (802) 864-7626.

Distributed to the US trade and internationally by Penguin Random House Publisher Services.

Berrett-Koehler and the BK logo are registered trademarks of Berrett-Koehler Publishers, Inc.

Printed in Canada

Berrett-Koehler books are printed on long-lasting acid-free paper. When it is available, we choose paper that has been manufactured by environmentally responsible processes. These may include using trees grown in sustainable forests, incorporating recycled paper, minimizing chlorine in bleaching, or recycling the energy produced at the paper mill.

Library of Congress Cataloging-in-Publication Data
Names: Citroën, Lida, author.
Title: The new rules of influence : how to authentically build trust, drive change, and make an impact / Lida Citroën.
Description: First edition. | Oakland, CA : Berrett-Koehler Publishers, Inc., [2024]
Identifiers: LCCN 2024007132 (print) | LCCN 2024007133 (ebook) | ISBN 9781523006663 (paperback) | ISBN 9781523006670 (pdf) | ISBN 9781523006687 (epub)
Subjects: LCSH: Leadership. | Influence (Psychology)
Classification: LCC HD57.7 .C5357 2024 (print) | LCC HD57.7 (ebook) | DDC 658.4/092—dc23/eng/20240404
LC record available at https://lccn.loc.gov/2024007132
LC ebook record available at https://lccn.loc.gov/2024007133

First Edition

32 31 30 29 28 27 26 25 24   10 9 8 7 6 5 4 3 2 1

Book production: Happenstance Type-O-Rama
Cover design: Ashley Ingram

*To all of us who want to know that by the
end of this crazy and wonderful journey
called life, we mattered, we made a difference,
and we left the world a better place.*

Contents

Preface

Why This Book?

Were you one of those kids in school who had lots of friends, always wore the cool backpack, and knew what to say to the cute boy or girl at parties?

I wasn't.

At 6'1", I've always stood out—literally. In the eighties in California where I grew up, there weren't many girls my height (who weren't supermodels), and I attracted attention for my stature. At age thirteen, I was the tallest person in my Catholic secondary school—including the teachers (some male)—as I topped 5'10".

Being so tall did come with some benefits: I would undoubtedly get looks when I entered a room, and if those times coincided with small bursts of adolescent confidence, I could project a grace and self-assuredness that, combined with my height, commanded positive attention.

But being tall—especially as a young woman—also came with challenges: I was uncoordinated and awkward with my long limbs and often was picked last for sports you'd think I'd excel at. Yes, basketball, I'm talking to you. Boys were intimidated by my height and avoided me like the plague. And, while I loved the look of high heels, wearing them would surely put me in nosebleed atmosphere territory, and I didn't have the self-confidence to pull that look off.

Empathetic people around me tried to encourage me to lean into what they saw as my God-given gift: "Stand tall and proud!" "Embrace your height!" "Your height is your unique quality—own it!" But I didn't feel those messages; I just wanted to be a "normal" height like the other girls.

I also wanted to be someone special, important, valued—someone who made a difference. I wanted my voice to matter and my opinions to be respected. Just because I physically stood out did not mean I knew how to harness my presence to be my authentic self and to have influence. Physical presence (and the attention that came with it) was not enough to exert influence. It was just a piece of what made me unique, like having red hair or freckles might.

After college, I spent twenty years navigating the corporate arena, which didn't do much to reinforce my understanding of influence. I saw people of diminutive stature—people who let others really see them, shared their passions and talents freely, and put themselves out there in bold and risky ways to defend their ideas—attract attention like I did for my height, but they wielded influence, while I didn't. I witnessed people whose command of the English language had me thumbing through the dictionary, while everyone else nodded with blissful enthusiasm. I noticed how people around me—people who were different from me in every conceivable way—were given free rein to explore their ideas and seemed to possess a secret sauce to influence that

I obviously lacked. When they sought to make change, they were successful.

What was I missing?

Later, like a good corporate soldier, I read all the books on leadership, executive presence, influence, confidence, and authority. I attended the seminars and workshops and meetings, took notes, and clapped madly; these new skills seemed so exciting! I practiced the techniques, bought the expensive tailored clothes, refined my communications, and sought to make a difference. All along, I felt I was playing a part, reading a script, and drinking from someone else's Kool-Aid fountain. None of it felt like it was coming from my heart.

As my career grew, I secured high-profile business development roles, met a lot of key decision makers from various industries, and participated in social and business initiatives and events. And my visibility in my community and industry grew. I'd even say my courage grew, but my impact still waned. I got things done. I was effective. I checked lots of "boxes," but I was also unfulfilled.

To those around me, I could seem like the epitome of confidence (my height helped here). I'm naturally quick on my feet, I have a sharp wit (yes, sometimes this can be problematic), and I'm well educated. And, sure, there were times I could assert myself into challenging situations, leveraging my expertise. But it wasn't consistent, internalized, or sustainable, and I can't say I always truly felt as confident or sure as I acted. In a sense, the books and seminars had worked: I knew how to pull off a self-assured presence, even if it wasn't authentic or heart-felt.

When I left Corporate America in 2008 and launched LIDA360, a personal branding and reputation management firm, my understanding of influence shifted in a seismic way. I knew my craft and my target audience, but for the first time in my professional life, I would have to embody all those qualities that the books and seminars and gurus had preached, not just project them. I would need to become influential if I was going to help others do so.

I began asking questions of the business owners I admired: What (and who) motivated and inspired them? Where did they find the most meaning and purpose in their work? How did they balance being genuine with being profitable? I listened to what they told me and tried the new skills on like a new pair of gloves: at first, they felt awkward and a bit stiff, but over time, the leather became supple, and the skills became embedded in who I was. For the first time in my life, I asked myself, *Could I be someone who truly motivated and inspired people? What is my purpose? What would being real, to me, feel like?*

Curious, I continued to learn. I watched people doing the work they loved, being the person they were most proud of, accepting the hard decisions, and embracing healthy choices. As I learned, my own voice grew. I found myself feeling more confident, not worrying about how it might *look* to be confident, but actually *feeling* self-assured. I offered my opinion, shared my skills and knowledge, and found myself attracting followers, clients, friends, colleagues, and communities, who, when surveyed, regularly described me as "warm," "inspiring," and "real." And my influence grew.

Over time, I found it almost easier to be me than to try to remember what I was supposed to be. I built a bigger followership online, attracting opportunities with my ideal target audiences, and grew more convinced that what I was doing now was what I was meant to do. This became my full and unwavering belief in myself and my offer.

I began working with clients who were influencers and thought leaders (in the truest sense of the words). They were changing the landscape of their industry and community, legislation, social narrative, and global issues. They were so deeply passionate about their area—whether it was advocating for neurodivergent individuals, coaching collegiate girls' hockey, helping obese patients change their lives, driving environmentally responsible real estate development, or advocating for the rights of marginalized immigrants—that it leaked from their pores. For them, not doing this work, and not being able to serve in the way they knew they were destined to serve, was simply not an option. Their sense of passion, commitment, and authenticity correlated to their influence.

Then I came across a quote attributed to Mark Twain, "There are two important days in your life: the day you are born, and the day you realize why." This rocked my world. This quote spoke to me in such a bold and profound way. It explained why I was so passionate about and committed to understanding the reason I was placed on this Earth, at this time, under these circumstances. I even shared it in my 2016 TEDx Talk, "The Power of Gratitude and Generosity: Serving Those Who Serve," as it seemed to explain my passion for serving the military.

I began to see that each of us has a purpose, which, once we identify it and lean into it, becomes non-negotiable for us. We can try to justify why fulfilling that purpose isn't practical—such as "It doesn't pay enough to work with at-risk youth. I'm better off as an accountant," or "I have to focus on providing for my family, even though serving communities in far-reaching corners of the world is what I'm called to do"—but we'll never feel fully fulfilled. We can learn to play a part, but that's not the same thing as living the part.

My voice developed more and more, along with my commitment to share an empowering message of hope and love and confidence with others. Over the years, I became an in-demand speaker and took international stages with joy and enthusiasm. I wrote books, articles, and blogs, and coached people to become more and do better. Life was on a roll!

The C-Word

And then Covid happened.

When we learned about Covid, life as we all knew it shifted. Covid gave us new language like "social distancing," "variants," "lockdown," and "doomscrolling," and we learned (as our mothers told us all those years ago) that washing our hands really does matter. We experienced isolation, loneliness, and mental health challenges and saw what the absence of human and social connectedness could do to our sense of well-being. Around the globe, we cheered for healthcare workers, panicked if we lost our sense of taste, and wondered what our world would look like once this was all "over."

Coming out of the pandemic, we slowly returned to "business as usual" and aimlessly migrated out of our yoga pants and into real shoes for the first time in eighteen months. But things had radically changed.

Leaders who recognized that paradigms had, in fact, shifted, knew that having meaningful influence with their teams meant leaning into real human needs, not running away from them. These leaders saw their peers face the backlash of sharing too much (or not enough) with audiences who valued their insights. They saw the threat and impact of cancel culture, as executives, entrepreneurs, and trailblazers embraced full transparency to reveal who they truly were—fears, warts, traumas, insecurities, and all.

These same leaders saw how people around them begged them to authentically build trust (instead of mandating compliance), to lead with humanity, passion, vulnerability, and impact (and not coerce others to follow their instruction). When leaders delivered on this need, people followed them—online and in person.

The need for more truth, connection, and empathy was amplified by the pandemic, but it didn't start there. The events of September 11, 2001, decades of global political unrest and uprising, the insertion of new language and considerations (such as pronouns to identify ourselves), and changes in how we work because of technology started before Covid and continue to morph even today.

But for me, the pandemic served as a demarcation in time to put into neon lights the fact that what worked before wasn't going to work going forward. People admitted to being more fatigued, less inspired, and more unhappy at work. My clients say their hobbies went from "hiking, biking, and sailing" to "gaming, gambling, and growing (weed)." Even today, years after Covid emerged, we don't surf outside—we surf online. Younger generations describe feeling social because of their collection of online "friends," but those aren't the people they spend physical time with on a Saturday afternoon. And still today, online communities scream for leaders and influencers to show their humanity and relate to people in real (unscripted) ways.

I realized that we need New Rules for how we engage with each other, reveal our humanity and vulnerability, and impact those around us. A TikTok video showing how to use puff pastry dough to make a delicious appetizer can go viral in seconds, while a heartfelt speech about the need to advance resources for marginalized communities falls on deaf ears. Surely there was a formula to build trust and make an impact, and I was committed to finding it.

Why I Wrote This Book

From the early days of my career, I've struggled with the traditional norms of executive presence. I listened to speakers, teachers, writers, and coaches talk about what it takes to succeed and exude confidence, and I saw one fatal flaw in the math: the examples tended to be men.

▸ You feel your power and influence have been marginalized.

▸ You're concerned that to have presence and influence means depreciating your authenticity.

▸ You have something important to share with the world and want to do more and be more.

My hope is that you internalize these New Rules as I have. Daily. I help my team live them. I've coached hundreds of clients to embody them. And I see the results: we all stand a bit taller, we raise our hands with more gusto, and we take the chances we know we're supposed to, because not doing so would feel soul-crushing and inauthentic. Our messages are received as intended. We're taken more seriously. Our voices are strong. We attract opportunities to lead and have impact. And, yes, some of us—even at 6'1"—now wear high heels as we speak our truth!

This is a struggle for a client I was hired to coach to greater levels of influence in his company. He's been so conditioned to be defensive—from his upbringing and the early part of his career—that he assumes others want to find fault with his thesis or reject him without considering his views. As a result, his senior leaders tell me, every discussion with him—from the mundane to the serious—feels like a battle. Even when he realizes they're all in the room just to touch base, it takes him a long time to trust that the other shoe isn't about to drop, keeping him in attack mode. "Is this his authentic, true voice?" they ask me.

After conversing and exploring the tools shared here with him, we find that there are ways to reframe his personal narrative (what he tells himself) about his deep need to feel he must protect himself. As I encourage him to do more questioning and listening at the outset of these conversations, the walls slowly start to come down.

Challenge your assumptions, then commit to and hold yourself accountable for continual growth, self-improvement, open-mindedness, and love. With new framing, you'll see more color, pattern, and texture in daily interactions and feel more acceptance, security, and warmth. And your message will be crafted to be the right one at the right time for the right audience.

To claim your voice, identity, and influence style, consider:

► When do you feel most peaceful, calm, and confident in discussing your ideas and vision?

► Who are your champions—the people who'll follow you, hold you accountable, and advance your vision?

▶ When do you feel the most angst or uncertainty positioning yourself, speaking up for your beliefs, or standing firm in your convictions?

▶ If you were your most real, true self, what would you sound like? How would you hold your body? Who would you surround yourself with?

Your voice, like your DNA, is uniquely yours. All you. Sure, the tapes and messages of our parents, friends, boss, community, and culture shape how our voice projects, but what you feel in your heart, in your head, and in your gut—and how you share that with others—is all you.

Should You Influence Others?

By now you're likely feeling excited about claiming your voice and being someone who can influence others. But just because you can, does it mean you should?

Amy's story rings true here. Amy had an impressive career for her young age, and her mentor, parents, and advisers encouraged her to go out on her own. Everyone around her recommended she run her own company as the one true way to capitalize on all she was capable of and have maximum influence over her market and career.

But Amy faced a challenge: she wasn't sure she *wanted* to be an entrepreneur. She wondered if there was another way to make a difference and asked me to help her sort it out.

We cataloged her skills. First, she was great at sculpting a business need or idea. She could, as she described it, "see around corners" and sense where a trend was headed. Working for various startups and private equity (PE) firms, she'd leveraged this talent to make other people a lot of money. She'd been brought into these firms early in their development and shored up the areas of the business where her strong opinions would be leveraged. Then, when the business right-sized or started to take off, she'd cash out and get recruited away. The PE firms loved her diverse background—from software (think early days of AI) to consumer goods to medical devices, she had a gift for growing opportunity.

Why wouldn't she do it on her own? Some suggested she could be an independent "hired gun" for companies or their investors, and she could swoop in and out of these emerging companies under the cloak of night, cashing her checks along the way.

"I just don't feel that having my own business would be fulfilling," she shared. She worried that such a high focus on transaction could take away the part she loved the most—seeing the idea, knowing who it would serve or benefit, and then bringing it to life. Yes, the money was great. But when she shared with me that she was using a lot of what she'd earned to fund her personal project— helping to end food deserts in the neighborhood she grew up in—the disconnect emerged: just because she could didn't mean she should. And just because she should (according to her advisers) didn't mean she *would*.

You must want to have influence. All the self-help books, well-intentioned advice from loved ones, and professional development tools in the world won't get you to take that step off the diving board and into the water if it's not in your heart to do so. That must come from you. You must feel, unequivocally and unapologetically, that you have a moral and personal obligation to do what you're meant to do, to be the person you're crafted to be, and serve in the way you're meant to serve. Then, and only then, should you raise your hand in the meeting, start a nonprofit, quit your job, or march in the streets. You'll need that kind of conviction and strength to do it.

Defining Influence

For those of you craving a bit of science talk here, the word *influence* originates from the Latin word *influere*, meaning to flow or stream into. Influence is, in fact and in practice, something we do, give, and teach so that others will do, give, and teach what we've shared. It's a quality we carry and possess, refine and communicate, and build over time. Influence flows from us to others so that it will flow to others from them. Okay, enough science talk.

The classic definition of *influence* is to sway a person, action, opinion, or course. Having influence means driving—directly or indirectly—the way something plays out. Some people call it "affect," and others refer to it as a force or quality that causes something to be or act in a way that might not have been originally intended. You can influence someone to think differently about an issue, choose a different toothpaste, or behave differently toward a population. Influence can lead us to follow someone that others follow (read: peer pressure) or resist calling out what seems blatantly obvious.

Some influence is situational—a doctor influences the patient's decision about whether surgery is needed—and some is more evergreen. You could argue that Maya Angelou, Jamie Dimon (of JPMorgan Chase), Nelson Mandela, Elon Musk, Malcolm X, and Princess Diana have been people of influence. Except for Jamie Dimon, I doubt any of them owned a red tie.

Defining Terms

Let's define some of the terms you'll read about in this book:

A person of influence These people live the New Rules. Sure, they have bad days like the rest of us, but their ability to spread their beliefs and views such that others want to follow them makes them a rare breed. We look up to them and admire how they live. Even under the microscope of social media or traditional media scrutiny, their influence is upheld. We believe the world is a better place with them in it, want to buy what they put their name to, and will get behind them to drive change.

Having influence This is what most of us can and will achieve. We stand up for our teammates and others trust us. We tell the company hard news, and they forgive us. We share the truth with our spouse, and they love us anyway. We have influence at work, at home, with friends, and online. Over time, having influence becomes a more solid foundation from which to operate—we can have influence within one community and then leverage it to grow our influence in another. This happens when someone known for being a leader in the tech sector, for example, pivots to sustainable investing, and their clients and staff go along.

There are also different types of influence, which map elegantly to different forms of communication:

Persuasive influence   As the name implies, here we use influence to convince someone of something. I want you to purchase this beachfront property, hire me, vote for me, or support my idea. I would use my persuasive skills to influence your buying decisions.

Demonstrative influence   When I influence you by showing you how to do something or by demonstrating why one option is better than the other when you're trying to make a decision, I'm using demonstrative influence. I'm taking the widget apart to show you how it's constructed, thereby influencing your opinion or beliefs about its quality.

Inspiring influence   This is the type of influence we love to see! This is Martin Luther King Jr. on the steps of the Lincoln Memorial talking about a better future, a world where we would all live in harmony. Evangelists, politicians, CEOs, and even parents can deploy inspiring influence to help us drive out evil, to teach us right from wrong, and to make us eat vegetables when chocolate sounds so much better.

Informative influence   Nuts-and-bolts influence, or informative influence, might seem less creative or inspiring, but it's more practical. The doctor explains why the procedure is in your best interest, and you agree to proceed. In this case, you are being influenced toward a choice or view because the information and data support that direction.

Influence Doesn't Come with Rank

Today, influence isn't relegated to people of a certain job title, gender, age, lifestyle, skin color, religion, or culture. In the last fifteen years, my client base, for instance, went from mostly men in corporate executive positions in US-based companies to entrepreneurs, social change and human rights advocates, teachers, athletes, and writers around the world. Women, young industrialists, celebrated athletes, content creators, professionals on the autism spectrum, LGBTQ+ people, and individuals navigating life with a disability began to seek my help to grow their influence and impact in bigger and more meaningful ways.

Perhaps the reason you've picked up this book is because you wonder if you, too, could have significant influence. Maybe you're wondering if now's the time for you to assert your opinion, lean into that new idea, or launch that movement that's been burning in your gut like gas station sushi. The need is there, the timing is right, and the ache is real—but are you the right person to champion this idea?

Influence emerges from all ranks and positions. While status and authority are often accompanied by title and position in the company or organization, that has all shifted, too. Today, people in all corners of the globe are resubscribing to their purpose and passion. I see junior accountants stand tall in company meetings and point out discrepancies in corporate philosophy (think "The Emperor's New Clothes"). I witness female doctors lean into their voice, dispelling their cultural narratives of "silence is golden," and assert their opinions in all-male board reviews. I see new entrepreneurs push back against their parents' values and chart a personal and professional path that previously took the courage of a fifty-year-old with a healthy IRA to pursue.

Admittedly, this new system of influence building challenges the thinking of those who embraced the older models. As generations of professionals stay in their jobs longer, and those around them begin to assert themselves differently, they also need to shift their thinking. The old system of coercion and compliance is replaced by collaboration, and this rocks some boats.

Working with a client who has been the boss for thirty years and done things one way, but now has to focus on diversity of thought and be open to new ideas and feedback, sometimes feels like doing brain surgery. No longer can these clients bark out orders or instructions or advice and expect not to be challenged. They must stop telling and start asking. While the process is painful at times (for both of us), the result is astounding. To see someone make the shift from "boss" to "leader" is breathtaking! They learn to empower and embrace, to be empathetic and real, and to watch others succeed where they've failed.

This new thinking helps institutionalize the need for the New Rules of building influence.

Can We Fake Influence?

Have you ever known a boss, a teacher, or a local politician who seems to present a canned message, who looks to the teleprompter on cue and shakes hands with just the right amount of enthusiasm to appear warm, but whom you wouldn't trust for a New York minute? If we're not paying close attention, we can mistake these people as having influence when we simply got influenced by them in the moment.

I see this play out on social media. Someone I follow, whose posts I enjoy, recommends a product—say, a shoe brand, mascara, or soda—and I feel compelled to buy it. Sometimes, without even thinking about it, I'll reach for my credit card because, "if it's good enough for her, it's good enough for me!" And a transaction occurs. Affiliate and influencer marketing at its best!

Being able to entice a fan or follower to a purchase is having influence over that person, but it's not exactly following the Rules as laid out in this book. It's transactional. New Rules–type influence is lasting, deep, scalable, and empowering.

As we move through this process together, we'll focus on all the ways you can genuinely show up as a person with influence to have influence when it matters. We'll reject the belief that influence, or presence, is a one-size-fits-all set of prescribed tactics. We're creating something bigger and more beautiful than any set of paint-by-numbers kit can produce. We're building a vision that's as unique and marvelous as you are!

I remember being asked to attend a job seeker workshop with a friend of mine who was between jobs. She didn't want to go alone, so I was enlisted as her "plus one." The only rule, she informed me, was that I was not allowed to speak up if I disagreed with the speaker (for fear of embarrassing my friend).

The presenter gave a thorough list of dos and don'ts for what to wear to a job interview to display power and confidence, as well as how to dress for success throughout your career. As she spoke, the audience frantically scribbled notes and made lists.

I struggled to maintain my promise to my friend, because the advice sounded like a 1950s book on how to be the ideal employee: "Limit your clothes to neutrals, like navy, white, tan, or ecru," she mandated. At this instruction, someone shot up their hand: "What's ecru? Is that like bone?" and so on. She offered these eager job seekers tips for how to not stand out (to avoid the risk of not fitting in), how to show their chameleon self, and how to be an attractive candidate the employer would view as moldable to their culture and company.

WTF?

Facing friendship suicide, I shot my hand up and asked, "But what if authentic to you is to wear bright colors and blue eye shadow and to express your personality with a sparkle or two?" The speaker replied, "Then you likely won't get the job," at which point my friend pretended not to know me.

"But is that such a bad thing?" I questioned. "If you had to work at a place that wanted ecru-clad workers, and you saw life in full color, would you be happy there?" I was asked to meet my friend in the parking lot and not participate in the rest of the workshop.

How to Use the Rules

The New Rules are not meant to be an à la carte menu of options for you to pick and choose according to your comfort level. They work as a well-orchestrated symphony of perfected synchronized instruments that empower you to be the unique person you are, share the mission and vision you care deeply about, and confidently influence those around you to move in your same direction.

As you deploy the Rules, you may find some harder to unpack and try on than others. In the past, it may have been easier to focus on your wardrobe, messaging, and data than on your own true voice and being real. You may have seen others commit to inclusivity and rolled your eyes. Maybe you listened to someone share a great, confident, and consistent story and wondered where they got it from. Over time, however, you'll focus less on what you're wearing, how you're standing, and who has the biggest title in the room, and more on how you can be all that you're meant to be.

CHAPTER 2

Discover Your *Why*

Why...

Be Courageous
and push past fear.

Be Real
and let others see
the true you.

Be Credible
to earn trust.

THE BIG IDEA: Inside each of us is a heart that beats. What's yours beating to? What drives you? When you have the courage to be yourself and act in accordance with your values, you can authentically build trust and credibility and leverage your humanness to make connection. Let's unpack what makes you real, special, unique, valuable, and trustworthy so you can empower others.

If the 1960s were about burning the bra, maybe this decade is about taking off the mask and letting our real colors shine through. While the self-help movement is credited with producing selfish and self-absorbed "everyone's a winner" offspring, it also made it okay to reflect, evaluate, and consider who we are as individuals—unique people with our own goals, fears, and characteristics.

Self-awareness is a practice many of us claim to be good at. "I check in with myself before any major decision," clients tell me. "I have a good radar for what's authentic to me and what's not," share others. When pushed, however, many of the business leaders, entrepreneurs, global professionals, and thought leaders I've had the honor of working with—who claim such deep levels of self-awareness—can't go that deep.

For example, have you considered how you'd respond to these self-reflections?

► **What would it look like for you to step into your truest, most authentic self?** Would you stand taller, dye your hair (or stop dyeing it), surround yourself with people unlike you, or speak with more confidence and deeper volume? Change your hard-to-pronounce last name? Wear high heels? What's stopped you from getting there?

► **Why do you do what you do?** No, I mean beyond that answer (the first and most politically correct answer). Go deeper. Why do you do your work, pursue your mission, work so darn hard, believe in your dream? Is it your vision or someone else's? Why do you believe you're meant to do that?

▸ **When you hit a roadblock, what gets you through it?** What's your modus operandi for moving through adversity and overcoming obstacles? Have you institutionalized that process in all aspects of your life or just at work?

▸ **Who inspires you at the more fundamental parts of your being?** Jesus? Oprah? Sir Richard Branson? Your dad? Your spouse? Why them? What qualities, characteristics, or behaviors do you believe they represent so fundamentally that they anchor into your values and drive you to being a better person?

Okay, those were some tough ones. And self-awareness is not just about answering questions like the good little students we are, but about internalizing those responses into our DNA such that we can't be separated from them.

If you don't have a clear picture of who you are, of what your voice is (and is designed to do), it's very difficult to inspire, motivate, and influence others.

Considering Your Why

To get us started, I'm going to ask something big and bold from you: you'll need to be unambiguous, unremorseful, and crystal-clear about your motivation, your *why*. Ready? Let's go.

Consider your motives. Are you seeking to influence because of, or for:

Fame?	Money?	Visibility?
Validation?	Power?	Respect?
Fear?	Idealism?	Independence?
Vengeance?	Status?	Recognition?
Love?	Approval?	Something (or someone) else?

Despite what your conspiracy theorist friends tell you, no one is watching you right now. . . . So, do the exercise and ask yourself (in your quietest "inside voice"): *Why do I want to be someone with influence?* Really ask yourself. Whatever your first answer is, reject it and go deeper. Then, go even deeper than that.

I remember a client asking me about my why after a long day of deep-thinking meetings around their business vision, purpose, passion, strategy, and more. I was exhausted from all the brain cells fluttering and synapses firing. We'd just sat down to dinner and, as my lovely cocktail was placed in front of me, my client asked, "Why do you do the work you do?"

Huh? I just really wanted to unwind from the mental gymnastics of the day. But I decided to respond.

"I want to be famous," I replied without missing a beat. "Oh! So, it's about ego!" he exclaimed, seemingly excited about cracking some mysterious code in my psyche.

"No," I replied. "I seek to be on as big a stage as I can get, because that means I can help the most people. I can speak a message that will show people who need my message how to be confident, happy, clear, and in control of their career and voice. Being known—fame—gives me that."

Now your turn: What's your why?

Why were you designed as you are right now, with the talents, hair color, IQ, muscles, abilities, blemishes, passions, accent, flaws, and experiences you have? What does it all mean for how you will help, lead, and serve others?

Oh, and if your answer is "money" or "fame" or the notoriety of it all, then you likely skipped forward in this book and are now realizing it's not the get-rich-quick book you were hoping for. I have no issue with money—I love money! But making money just for the sake of accumulating wealth is not influence.

You might answer:

▸ To honor my father's legacy

▸ To help children with disabilities the way I was helped

▸ To show young Hispanic girls a role model who looks like them, comes from their same background, and is thriving in fashion design

▸ To stand up for the rights of marginalized people who can't advocate for themselves

▸ To heal people who couldn't afford to hire me

▸ Because I was created by God to serve in this way, in this role

▸ Because I'm grateful for those who sacrificed so much for my freedom

▸ To help others succeed where I had advantage to help me

▸ To help my team finally get the credit and respect we deserve

Or whatever comes from your heart and lights your path.

Aligning Your Voice and Passion

When we clarify our motives—I mean really clarify!—we can align our heart, head, and gut with what's needed to project our purpose to others. This is where we find our voice, our direction, and our why. Then, it becomes less about the discomfort of self-promotion, and more about an unwavering need to lead the way we are designed to, to lean in when it feels uncomfortable, and to love in the most whole, unconditional, and real way imaginable.

When we strip away the "shoulds" and the "supposed tos" from how we see our role in this world, our raw purpose is exposed. Influence thrives here! It's where we feel most confident, authentic, and impactful. It's from here that we can build trust and drive change. When we stop trying to be authentic and just are authentic, when we stop worrying about looking the part and just become the part, our voice is more natural, our purpose is easier to share, and our impact is evident.

Try it. Just try asking yourself who you are and why you are. Not your job title, rank, or status, and you don't need to think of this from a spiritual or religious vantage point. You are unique and different, and everything you've done so far has led you to reading these exact words, right now. Why is that?

Your Origin Story

When considering your why, it can also be helpful to look at your origin story: How did you get here? Own your origin story because, like your DNA, it's unique to you.

Perfect and flawed and strong and amazing. Unpack for your own edification why you do what you do. Is it because your parents came to the US to give you and your siblings a better shot at success and happiness, and you saw how hard that was for them? Is your drive and passion stemming from this story?

Or did you leave an abusive marriage, and for the first time in your life you needed to get a job and support yourself because you chose freedom and safety over comfort? What challenges did you endure? What successes did you achieve? What did you learn?

Or were you raised in a typical middle-class suburban family, participated in the normal extracurricular activities, earned your Girl Scout or Boy Scout badges on schedule, and decided later that you wanted something different? That you wanted to serve others who had less or limited access?

Your origin story—where your story begins—is unique to you and is exactly as it should be. Whether you had to endure hardship to be the person you are today, or you were given advantages and now want to share what you know and have with others, your story is yours.

A veteran I coached had a remarkable origin story. He was born in a poor part of West Africa during highly turbulent political and economic times. His parents, unable to care for him, put him up for adoption. When he was five years old, an unlikely scenario played out and he was adopted by a Caucasian family from suburban Wisconsin. Growing up in his new community, he told me, he never saw kids (or anyone) who looked like him or shared his background.

He later joined the military, where he suddenly felt like part of a group. He was surrounded by diversity of appearance, culture, language, and style. It was there that he flourished and started loving who he was becoming. He adored his adoptive parents, but as a young Black boy with a strong African accent in suburban Wisconsin, life had been challenging. Upon leaving the military in his forties, he made it his mission to help other children who'd been adopted by loving parents of a different faith, culture, race, background, and so on, find connection and community. His origin story made his purpose and mission relatable, memorable, and compelling, even if you never experienced anything similar in your life.

Your why is crucial to your influence process. Write it down, etch it into your piano (funny childhood story about that one . . . but that's for another time), tattoo it on your wrist, add it to your mousepad, or tell your friends. When you get to your why, keep it close and remind yourself of it when things get tough and you're tempted to retreat.

As I'm writing this book, I sat with a client of mine discussing her why and origin story. Today, she is a formidable force in social activism, publicly advocating for the voices of the marginalized communities she represents. Her career has been filled with trials and tribulations that would make even a career politician blush—and she's been resilient and persistent at every step.

"I've always felt an unwavering commitment to serve," she explained. "My parents and community growing up taught me that the world is a big place, but it's small in how we help and care for each other. Even as a young adult, I was never the person who could just walk past someone who needed help. I just physically couldn't."

Early in her career, she wasn't clear about whether she wanted the leadership roles she later gained, but she knew she wanted to drive change. Whatever way that meant for her, she was in.

In her most contentious role, where she led an organization of thousands of people advocating for justice and rights and fairness, not only did she find herself a minority in the room (she was one of few women in meetings, and the only one who'd achieved the leadership title) but she also saw instances of voices being discounted and abandoned as others sought to protect themselves (and their egos) at all costs.

"I'm not afraid of having the difficult conversations," she shared. "I think to have influence you [can't] be. While I'm more comfortable asking questions in tense situations, I strive to reserve judgment and focus on inclusivity to drive the conversation. Everyone has a game plan, even me. It's just that my game plan is a strong belief in humanity, not self-gain or self-preservation."

Her passion to serve those she's served has cost her. She's received public scrutiny, been thrown out of politicians' offices, and had her personal life relentlessly dissected. But these are sacrifices to get her closer to the purpose she feels she's on this earth to fulfill. Her why is clear, enduring, and resilient.

RULE 1: BE COURAGEOUS and Push Past Fear

Rule 1 may be the scariest thing you do.

To promote your vision and your voice, to stand out in front and show your soft underbelly to the naysayers and the haters and the online trolls, you'll have to display personal agency, be bold and willing to embrace risk, and be shamelessly brave. Simple, right? Not even close.

Courage means when you believe in a cause, solution, or effort, you go forward with gusto and conviction. Courage is not the absence of fear. We can be afraid—scared even—and remain courageous in how we pursue our vision.

I've worked with some of the most courageous individuals—people whose names you might not know but who've designed groundbreaking technologies, started companies, related to disparate audiences, and physically fought wars—but many of them wouldn't describe themselves as courageous. They've done what they believed needed to be done. Or felt was the right thing to do. Or what others wouldn't do. And they moved forward into the battle or the threat or the vast unknown without safeguards or training wheels; they just did it because not doing it wasn't an option.

Maybe you're reading this and thinking, *I'm not trying to change the world. I just want my boss to listen to me when I speak up.* And that's great. You need to have courage, too. You'll need to be able to raise your hand and offer your insights, ideas, or objections when your boss is in a bad mood or when you're not sure your idea is fully baked or when you wonder if you've earned the right to speak up in that meeting.

You'll need to be courageous enough to point out the flaws in your boss's or politician's or parents' reasoning, because you see something they can't or won't see. Perhaps you represent a community someone is trying to relate to, but they're missing the mark. Do you have the courage to point this out? Will you offer to help coach them if you believe their message and vision has validity?

Your courage will drive your influence. You must believe in yourself and your message even when others don't, or when they are skeptical and question your reasoning. Particularly when you ask others to have faith in you, you'll need to project your courage. If you look uncertain, they will question you. When you have courage, you drive courage in them to take a chance on you.

Being courageous might mean:

▸ Speaking up in a meeting (when you feel insecure)

▸ Using your own voice and not relying on the data, insights, or opinions of others to make your case (when you worry if you've earned the right)

▸ Stepping onto the stage to share your message (when you fear public speaking)

▸ Changing your style to be more "you" (when it's easier to conform to the predominant style of others)

▸ Taking on a cause or initiative that has high visibility (when you fear it may cost you friends or social standing)

▸ Being vocal on an issue that gnaws at you (but which could cost you your job)

▸ Asking yourself hard, deep, and personal questions (when you fear what you might learn about who you are and what you're capable of)

As a child, I loved *The Wizard of Oz*. I was enamored with the tale of Dorothy and the ruby slippers and finding her sense of home again. What I never understood fully at the time, however, was the power of her new friends, the Scarecrow (who's searching for a brain), the Tin Man (who's looking for a heart), and the Cowardly Lion (who's lacking courage). We learn through the story that without these important qualities, Dorothy's new friends are unfulfilled and unhappy. When they find that missing piece, they are complete and full of optimism and joy.

The Cowardly Lion is a juxtaposition and irony in himself: he's a big strong lion, yet he's afraid and timid. When he needs to serve others—to help Dorothy find her way home—he starts to find what he's missing, and his courage grows.

Influence works like this, too. We get influence by giving influence. And sometimes, you have to display a bit more courage than you feel in the moment. You may have to project "lion" when inside you feel "kitten," but you do so because your message and vision require you to be courageous. In your service to others, as you advance and promote your vision and ideas, your courage (and thereby your influence) will take root.

When you share what you know, as you stretch out past your skis and get uncomfortable, when you lean into fear and self-doubt, you grow your courage muscle. You learn that it's not about being perfect, but about having conviction. It's not about knowing everything but about knowing yourself. Courage comes from facing what scares you (an intimidating boss, imposter syndrome, negative self-talk, the unknowing, your own tail) and moving forward anyway because you believe with every cell in your body that you were meant to do, share, give, and impact others in this way.

When Warren Buffett candidly highlights what he's learned from his many mistakes, instead of solely touting his business acumen and success, he encourages others to be courageous and take risks. When Steve Jobs stood on stage in front of investors, consumers, a skeptical media, and the world to introduce us to the iPhone, he showed courage in his vision. When my client stood before her organization's leadership and took the slings and arrows on behalf of the people she represented, to advocate for new rules and processes to ensure their safety and protect their voice, she showed courage.

Courage isn't guaranteed to make you popular, famous, celebrated, or followed. It is one rule among ten that you must follow and internalize to become the person of influence you're meant to be.

Questions to ask yourself:

- ▶ When do I show courage? Am I able to identify the times, experiences, situations, and conditions under which I can be courageous?

- ▶ When I feel myself restricting my courage and maybe going along with others for the sake of conformity, or holding back my views because of potential retribution, what could help me feel more courageous?

- ▶ Who, in my life or career, displays the kind of courage I admire? What can I learn from them as I grow toward building influence?

Courage is not an end state. You don't one day check a box and say, "Got it; now I'm courageous." It's a fluid process that grows with experience, validation, maturity, and confidence. Look for examples of people who display courage and watch them. What are they doing and saying that tells you it's true courage, not just preparation and stage presence? Then, put one foot in front of the other and embark on your own authentic, unique journey to be courageous.

RULE 2: BE REAL and Let Others See the True You

When choosing what to call this rule, I wrestled with using the word *authentic* or *genuine*. Let me explain why I chose *real*.

The word *authentic* has certainly grown in popularity. Presenters preach authenticity from the stage, books are written about "how to be authentic," and studies showcase the efficacy of authenticity in the workplace, politics, and society. In fact, in 2023, it was Merriam-Webster's "Word of the Year." (Not sure if it got a crown and sash, but it made quite a splash.)

But, I asked myself, does that mean *authentic* is the right choice for this important rule? Is it trendy, widely understood, and actionable, or is it like gravitas—we know it when we see it, but we can't really describe how to get it. This is what I wrestled with.

Real, on the other hand, seems to be more widely understood, even though it lacks some of the modern glamor of *authentic*. We instruct someone to "be real," "keep it real," or to "get real" when we're asking for their truest self, the unscripted and raw version of who they are and who we need to see. And, for most of us, "getting real" indicates heartfelt, true, and deep clarity. When someone is angry with us, for example, and they're trying to choose their words carefully for fear of hurting our feelings, and we have no clue what they're saying, we may encourage them to give us the real reason for their upset. We ask them to "be real" and speak from their heart. When the CEO takes to the podium to let employees know the company is in trouble, they typically don't say, "I'm going to get authentic here," but they may say, "I'm going to get real with you all." For these reasons, I chose *real* for this rule.

Being real necessitates a rawness, a truth, and vulnerability. When you hear the word *vulnerable*, what comes to mind? Do you imagine a mushy, emotionally exposed, and overly expressive person? Someone you'd feel obligated to indulge in heart-wrenching and deep introspections, and whom you fear won't stop sharing their most personal inner thoughts?

That's old-school thinking.

Being real, vulnerable, and genuine is core to building influence. If you can't share who you are, what you feel, what you need, and what you believe, how are we to trust that what you tell us or ask us to do is good for us?

I believe when real people show realness, we can see it a mile away. We might envy them, admire them, or fear them, but we can truly see them.

I learned this recently from a client of mine. I've worked with clients going through trauma—either at their own doing or not—and seen many examples of courage to be real as they push through. But Amanda showed me something unexpected.

A passionate and confident woman, Amanda had been a victim of bullying and cyberattacks the likes of which I'd not seen before, at least not to this extent. The online trolls and reputation sabotage she endured at the hands of people who'd worked with her, hired her, and previously supported her were shocking. She was accused of everything from embezzlement (from her previous employer, clients, and colleagues) to sexual misconduct with clients—neither of which had any truth or basis in fact. Stunned from the degree and severity of the attacks, she'd enlisted PR teams, lawyers, and therapists to try to navigate the situation, only to find herself circling the toilet bowl of human behavior daily.

I wasn't even sure I could help Amanda or wanted this kind of vitriol in my own life. I worried that I could easily become part of her assault, just as other people who had aligned to try to help her had been. Ultimately, we decided to work together to try to get her life, career, and reputation back. It was not an easy goal.

Months after we began our work, with a personal brand and reputation repair framework in hand, her positioning strategy clearly outlined with timelines and checkboxes, and goals on Post-it notes posted around her office, Amanda started to emerge from the darkness. Then came a real test: she was tapped to speak at a large conference for her former industry. She was certain some of her old colleagues and naysayers would be there, and the idea paralyzed her.

We talked through pros and cons, we evaluated risks and upsides, and we planned for a confident and calm response should she be confronted with the negativity and hate while onstage. She was prepared, assured, and ready. And I was certain she'd cancel at the last minute. I knew how this terrified her, and while I could pump her up with praise and tools, she'd have to do the hard work.

I sent her a text the morning of the speech wishing her luck, giving her support, and adding a few charming emojis to lighten the stress. She shot back the "terrified face" emoji, and again, I expected her to invent a last-minute emergency.

Instead, hours later she wrote, "I did it! I really did it! I stood in my truth and spoke from my heart! And it worked!"

She'd taken the stage and looked at the audience, at each person judging her and evaluating how she'd handle herself after such public and lasting scrutiny and harassment. And she judged them right back. She had been her most real and shared a personal message of strength, conviction, power, and authenticity that disarmed the audience and won them over to her side. She wasn't scripted; she laughed and cried at all the same times as her audience. Her realness was visible to everyone. Her voice was strong and human, marking a potent step in her regaining her place in her world and career.

Realness and Transparency Aren't the Same Thing

An important point: I believe there's a fundamental difference between being real and being transparent. Put aside the dictionary for a moment and follow me here. Being real is letting people see you, hear you, and know you. It's showing your vulnerable side and trusting that your audience won't abuse or hurt you because of it. Realness dictates that if you're asked a question or you volunteer an idea or opinion, you're being truthful in your response. If you weigh in and share a belief, it's one you truly hold. Your realness, tested and witnessed over time, builds authentic trust.

Transparency, on the other hand, is letting everything hang out—sharing every thought, idea, belief, fear, dream, rash, or trauma you've ever experienced with the world. This is risky. Yes, you should be transparent about your reasoning as you make an argument ("I believe we need to advocate for changes in the workplace to support neurodivergent employees. Here's why . . ."), but as individuals, we are allowed to keep some things private. We do not have to share experiences in our past that we're not comfortable making public. We do not have a social obligation to weigh in on every topic in the news or on social media. If we decide to offer an insight or opinion, it should be real for us, but we also retain the right to withhold our view if keeping that private is right for us.

I've had clients who stressed about how to react and what to say when the 2022 US Supreme Court overturned *Roe v. Wade*. They felt that (as a lawyer, a woman, a brother/mother/father/sister, a Christian, etc.) they had a duty to chime in with their thoughts. But some of these individuals had trauma associated with their viewpoint or didn't feel comfortable sharing their views publicly and worried about what to do. My advice to them was clear: if you feel that commenting on the decision is aligned with who you really are, if you're comfortable sharing those views, and if sharing your views will drive a vision you're passionate about advocating for, then do so with clarity and confidence. If your desire to jump into the conversation is based on a fear of missing out or being targeted for a lack of viewpoint, that's high school peer pressure and we're too old for that nonsense.

Being real is when you show us who you really are (gray hairs, dreams, failures, and all)—when you let us know *you*. Now, before you jump on me, an experienced executive who just *must* have gray hairs and more than a few wrinkles that sometimes get airbrushed out, let me remind you: it's okay to want to show your best self to others. If you feel good smoothing out a few blemishes before posting a photo, go for it. If dyeing your hair makes you feel more confident in your work, I see no harm. But when someone asks you a real and honest and hard question, you don't get to "phone a friend" and ignore the opportunity to share your truth. If you answer the question, you must do so with realness.

What does being real mean to you?

For some, it may mean coming out of the closet or owning past mistakes or addressing their dreams head on. For others, it could mean replying from the stage, "I don't know that answer," to an obvious question. For the rest of us, it may mean being more honest and vulnerable and raw than we have in the past.

I remember a few years back when I was trying to create more video content because I saw it as a way to share different messages in ways other than just text and graphics. Typically, I'd record a video and send it off to my marketing manager, and she'd add graphic elements (like my logo) and subtitles.

One day, I recorded a more personal message on video. I still had my hair styled right, my lashes glued on, and ideal lighting, but instead of sending the video off to be "prettied up," I just posted it. I even acknowledged in the text part of the post that I'd been so excited to share this personal (and hopefully inspiring) message that I jumped over my normal process.

The result was incredible—the realness and approachability of the message resonated. People commented that the message was powerful and raw and exactly what they needed. In my head, I worried that I'd abandoned my typical script of having something more visually appealing before posting, but what I learned was that the real message sometimes needs to be shared in its most un-prettied-up way.

Realness for you might be:

▶ Speaking from your heart in a meeting, instead of relying on the data

▶ Asking the questions no one else will ask

▶ Going against what your parents, spouse, friends, boss, or community thinks is best for you

▶ Challenging commonly held assumptions

▶ Betting on yourself

▶ Sitting at the conference room table in the meeting instead of along the back wall

▶ Wearing color instead of corporate neutrals

Realness and Self-Awareness

Being real means being clear about who you are, what you want and need, and why you're here.

When I teach programs about self-awareness, I like to start by asking the audience how many of them consider themselves to be self-aware. Not self-actualized or self-absorbed or self-centered, but truly aware of how they are, who they are, and why they are.

Most hands go up.

Most people have read the self-help books and attended the rallying seminars that promise fulfillment and a true sense of clarity around purpose—and most people go back to their day jobs questioning why it all matters.

If we accept the definition of self-awareness as the ability to clearly see who you are; why you behave, react, love, and communicate the way you do; and how your beliefs, perceptions, values, emotions, and thoughts shape you, then it's no wonder that it can take a lifetime to get to this level of deep introspection.

Being real requires a high degree of self-awareness. It's not right to just go through the motions to display credibility, to tell people to trust you, and to claim you're being an authentic, confident leader when you're not any of those things. You can't claim realness if you aren't aware of who you are, at the core.

Realness Is Scary

When we show our real selves to others, we let them see us. They see us for who we are, not who we believe we should be. Think about that: Have you ever considered how much of what you do, say, dress like, and believe is because someone told you that's what's "right" or "acceptable"? Have you taken the time to consider if it's right or acceptable *for you?*

To this day, I struggle to wear a sleeveless blouse to a meeting or presentation because in my ear are my high school teachers saying that "ladies should cover their shoulders." Yes, I'm more comfortable without long sleeves, but pushing through that small, insignificant barrier has proven challenging. When in doubt, I default to the messages I was taught about what I "should" do, rather than fully leaning into what I want to do, what feels most like me. Have you done that too?

Being real means you're clear on what you need, who you are, and what your purpose is. You then embrace the fear, excitement, and love you have so you can do your thing. If that means starting a business, you do it. If that means not working the way your predecessor did, you challenge your job description. If that means asserting yourself among your male colleagues because you're just as competent and qualified and passionate as they are, then you do it.

The good news here is that you no longer need to script out every message and have AI tools filter your photos and expect that others will blindly trust that who you are is who you say. People relate to people who are real, and real people are flawed and quirky and human. Just like those who'll follow them. Being able to show those flaws is key to having influence.

Questions to ask yourself:

- ▸ When I'm being real around others, do I feel empowered or scared?

- ▸ Why do I resist being real when I know that I should be?

- ▸ Who do I know who's consistently real with me? What can I learn from them?

- ▸ The last time I felt the temptation to be real but resisted, what was happening and why did I refrain?

Being real takes practice and commitment. It will always be easier and feel safer to script yourself, check the prescribed boxes, and follow the party line, but that's not why you're here. You're ready to show people who you are and have them see the passion, commitment, and realness in your eyes and hear it in your voice. You can do this!

RULE 3: BE CREDIBLE to Authentically Earn Trust

When Elizabeth Holmes, the biotech founder of the blood therapy company Theranos who was later convicted of defrauding investors, purposefully lowered her vocal tenor to sound more confident and acceptable, did that raise her credibility? No. Not at all. When actress Amber Heard dressed in all black to represent her seriousness in her lawsuit filings against former partner Johnny Depp, did she project more trustworthiness? Nope. Nada. Zilch.

Credibility doesn't come from dressing or sounding the part, but from something far more meaningful: when we can clearly articulate who we are and what we stand for and then demonstrate that we consistently live our values, we earn credibility.

Thousands of books have been written on the topics of integrity, honor, credibility, and trust. While being influential means others will rely on you, believe you, find you credible, and follow you into the future, you'll need to demonstrate authentic credibility to have lasting impact.

The Credibility Formula: Values + Actions = Credibility

Earning credibility is not just about optics or spin or word-smithing. To be a person with credibility, you must follow this powerful and potent formula: values plus actions earns credibility. This formula is non-negotiable. There are no shortcuts, workarounds, AI tools, or cheat sheets to navigate it. This is the only formula that works. Let's examine it more closely.

Being credible requires you to be clear in your values. Values are what you stand for—believe in so fundamentally that they are at the core of your being—and are personal to you. Your values are yours—not those of your parents, or your spouse, or your social media influencers. Your values must be owned by you such that if they were to be removed, you wouldn't be you.

Your values guide how you act and evaluate situations; they empower you to decide right and wrong, good and bad, yes and heck no! When you are aligned with your values, you feel real, whole, confident, and clear about who you are and why you're here. Even the toughest choices (which job to accept, when to speak up, how to walk away) run through your values, whether or not you're aware of it.

While it might sound simple, values work is hard. Begin by thinking about what you stand for and when you've been faced with tough decisions or obstacles: What is the moral code you leaned on to help you through? Your values are in there. Write down the words, feelings, thoughts, and sentiments that swirl around your values. Put them through the sieve until just a few values emerge—clear, shiny, and obvious to you. Those values are your superpowers. They make you who you are, and when put into action, they give you credibility.

Actions, the second step in the credibility formula, must demonstrate consistency with values. If you're offering someone feedback, for example, and honesty is a core value of yours, then the recipient must experience your feedback as direct and unadulterated. But what if they don't understand that you're being so blunt because you value honesty? If they wonder about your motives or perceive you to be mean and hurtful, they won't assign you credibility for your honesty value. There should be no question in that person's mind that you're offering input and insight based on your placing importance on honesty. Which is why you need to tell them. You need to take the reins of your credibility by setting the context, explaining, "I realize what I'm about to share with you might feel harsh. But I value honesty, at all costs. So here goes." Now the value and the action are aligned.

Actions must align in both your mind and the minds of the people you want to influence. When others see that you "walk the talk" and live by your values, they can learn to authentically trust you. They may not like what you stand for or how you behave, but the connection between values and action earns you credibility.

Think of someone you know who you'd say is credible. What do you know about that person? Do they show you different personalities and behaviors depending on their mood? Or are they the same whether they're happy or sad, winning or losing?

For you, credibility might look like:

▶ Being careful about the promises you offer and make, knowing it will be vital that you honor each of them.

▶ Telling your peers that you can't join them for an outing because that event doesn't align with your beliefs. While it would be easier to just RSVP "no, thanks" or come up with an excuse like "I need to wash my dog," sharing your values teaches them to authentically trust you.

▶ Turning down a promotion because the new role conflicts with your personal goals, such as requiring you to be away from home instead of with your new baby.

▶ Refusing to remain silent as members of your community are publicly ridiculed or harassed, as your values of advocacy and justice gnaw at your soul.

▶ Going against public opinion because your beliefs drive you in a different direction.

Credibility and Integrity

If you heavily salt someone's food and they begin drinking water like a camel, does that mean you influenced them? Sure. You did something that caused a reaction.

But influence isn't about cause and effect. I can kick your shin and you'd say "ow!" but that isn't influence (and isn't nice, either!). Influence relies on a buy-in from the other person, a willingness to be influenced into an action, belief, or behavior.

Credibility is a key to building influence. While my neighbor can mow my lawn and that makes me happy, they didn't necessarily influence me into thinking more positively of them. If I know that neighbor to be selfish, loud with their music at night, and unhelpful in general, one act of kindness likely won't change my view. The act of mowing my lawn without being asked was kind, but it doesn't build their influence or credibility with me.

Integrity drives credibility and builds authentic trust. Someone with integrity is known to have a solid moral compass. They are honest, they're self-aware, and they have a clear sense of what's right and what's wrong. They live their life through the lens of moral rightness and follow both the Golden Rule (do unto others as you'd like done unto you) and the Platinum Rule (listen for how others need to be treated, even if that's not what you'd want).

The person with integrity doesn't seek out fame or credit or recognition for doing the right thing. They do it simply because it's right. A behavior or action might be part of their job, like a fireman's duty to run into the burning building to save a child, but they do it more because it's what's right to do even when no one is watching.

Someone out of alignment with their values lacks integrity. This person is different in different situations. For one group, they might promote a set of clearly defined principles, but in another setting, they show support for the opposition. They claim to value and stand for something that's popular or trending, but when the tides of popular sentiment shift, they're out of there faster than a long-tailed cat in a room full of rocking chairs.

I've known people with a lack of integrity. They will tell you one thing and then later, when asked about it, claim it never happened. They get through on their charm, looks, social skills, or wealth, but below the surface there's nothing lasting to speak of. These people typically end up craving attention at any cost.

A boss who'll sacrifice their team for their own career advancement is one example of someone who lacks integrity. Have you ever worked for someone who was quick to accept credit for your work and ideas, but blamed you and your colleagues when things went sideways? Have you heard of politicians who'll throw the other side of the aisle under the bus when their idea doesn't pass and get funded? "We tried to help you!" they'll tell their constituents, knowing full well their idea never stood a chance, just made for good sound bites.

When someone tells us to trust them, then lets us down; when they say they've "got our back" but put their self-interest ahead; or when they say they understand how we feel and won't do it again but then do, there's a lack of integrity.

I worked for a boss like this once. He was fabulous at offering promises and reassurances. "I've got you," he'd frequently say. The problem was, when pressed or under scrutiny, he was the first one to claim he had no prior knowledge. There were times I'd wanted to stretch outside my comfort zone professionally. Afraid to go too far,

I'd ask for his guidance and counsel. His advice seemed spot-on, and I appreciated that he appeared to mentor me as I grew my career. When I was successful, he stood proudly next to me, embracing "our" success. When I failed, he was nowhere to be found.

Over time, I became skeptical of his advice. Could he be trusted? Did he have my best interests at heart? Was he listening to my ideas and selling them behind my back? He'd earned a lack of integrity with me and could no longer be trusted to influence or inspire me. My commitment to his success diminished, my job satisfaction fractured, and I changed jobs.

Tapping into Your Integrity

To be a person with integrity, you need to clearly establish credibility and then consistently behave in alignment with who you profess to be. This process is neither swift nor easy, but it's one that has lifelong positive impact when done correctly.

An ingredient in integrity is honesty, and this might be partly why the integrity nut is so hard for us to crack. Are you honest? Is your honesty situational or conditional? Are you honest on your taxes, but lie to your wife about where you were last night? Are you honest with your boss but give your team artificial deadlines to make them work harder? Are you honest with your partner, but lie to your accountant about when you mailed their check?

Most clients tell me they're honest. They strive to be honest in the way they represent themselves and speak to others. When challenged, though, many of them sugarcoat feedback instead of being direct for fear of upsetting their direct reports. Or they hide the fact that they didn't really have family in town over the weekend, they just didn't want to go into the office. Or they get confused about the differences around honesty, truthfulness, directness, candor, and so on. Whichever word you choose to describe the practice of telling someone the truth as you know it to be, you'll need to own your ability to be honest and live an honest life to have integrity.

Integrity is not something you can make so because you say it. Years ago, I authored an article titled "Telling Me to Trust You Is Like Saying You're a Good Kisser. It's Really Up to Others to Say." In the piece, which ended up going viral, I wrote about all the ways we often try to shortcut the trust-building process by professing our values yet not living them. When we have more instances of inconsistency than consistency and of not being a person others would describe as authentic or impactful, it's virtually impossible to build authentic trust and be seen as having integrity.

Want to know just how valuable integrity is? Type the word *integrity* into Google, followed by any business type or profession (insurance, auto repair, realtor, pilot, politician, coaching, author), and see how many thousands of results there are. If only we could bottle integrity—we'd all be bazillionaires!

When You Fail the Integrity Test

Personally and professionally, one of the biggest challenges around values and building credibility, is when we must choose to stand true to them even when they're incompatible with popular opinion, social sentiment, or even job security. When we stand for what we believe in—wholeheartedly—we can face the demons of scrutiny, backlash, and criticism head-on.

This is certainly where I've failed.

I've always prided myself on having a good moral compass. Whether you call it integrity or faith or just being a good person, as long as I can remember I've sought to always do the right thing, regardless of who's watching.

I got tested on this in my first real management job. Throughout my career I'd led plenty of teams, initiatives, committees, and groups, but managing people as part of my job was new to me. I was hired to manage a team of four professionals, and then within three months and two corporate reorganizations, I had ten people reporting to me. I had no clue that there was a difference between being an inspiring and empowering leader and being a tactical manager who reviewed timesheets, approved PTO, and negotiated bickering between direct reports.

Even those were skills I could have learned and embraced. It was the one that made me compromise my values that brought on an ulcer and deep moral conflict. I supervised a manager who had been with the company a long time; was well liked, social, and friendly; and had just started a family with his wife. To me, he was pleasant and seemed open to feedback and input. The problem was that my boss wanted me to get rid of him.

I asked about the reasoning and was told "He's not performing up to par," blah blah blah. I spotted the headlights off in the distance and saw the trainwreck coming. I had to be the one to get rid of a well-liked company asset and would be viewed negatively for it.

But this is business, right?

It was how my boss wanted me to get rid of him that made me question everything about my job and organization. The company knew that termination would be costly, as he'd been a team member a long time. Getting him to quit was far more cost-efficient, and so I was taught how to get someone to quit with death by a thousand cuts.

I was instructed to begin giving him unrealistic deadlines, then reprimand him for missing them or asking for delays. I left him off important communications, putting him in the uncomfortable and embarrassing place of not being able to participate fully in meetings. I asked him to work later hours, cutting into his time with his wife and young son. With each technique I was taught, my stomach and heart hurt more and more.

But this is business, right?

When the day finally came, he tearfully walked into my office and resigned. I felt like quitting with him. My heart broke and I felt disgusted with myself. How could I treat someone like this? Sure, I was doing as I was told, but is this right? I went against my values and what I believed was right—and that was wrong, in all ways. In that moment, I vowed never to compromise my values again. I was also instructed not to share, vent about, or express the process I'd participated in or I'd risk retribution by the company.

Today, what I was instructed to do would surely be characterized in companies as "bullying" and not tolerated. It's been years since I left my corporate career, in part because of practices like this. To this day, I wish more than anything I'd have had the courage to stand up for my values, to spit in the face of unfair treatment and apologize to that manager and his family.

Living Our Values

Two values I hold dear are gratitude and generosity. When I'm faced with a business prospect, volunteer opportunity, new relationship, or chance to share my voice, I ask if I will feel grateful and generous in the process. If I won't, it's not a great move for me. When I can or suspect I will be able to, I'll pursue it. Over the years, my dedication to serving military veterans and military families, my commitment to mentoring women in business and social entrepreneurship, and my dedication to my clients (long after the term of my contract expires) stand as testaments to my values.

But I also have an obligation—as you do—to connect the dots and remind those I'm serving why I am doing so. This part feels icky, yes. Knowing how easy it is for someone to misunderstand or come to the wrong conclusion about why you're doing what you're doing means you need to spell it out for them. You'll need to say (as do I) why you're doing the action—which value of yours is leading this behavior or relationship. Then, instead of being skeptical or misreading the situation, others will be clear that your why (value) is directing your action (what).

Questions to ask yourself:

▸ What are my core values? Really core, not the list that goes on my résumé. What are the unwavering values I won't or can't deviate from?

▸ How can I resist the temptation or pressure to compromise my values? When the stakes are high (kids to feed, medical bills to pay, social media scorn), how will I lean into what I know is right, regardless of the risk to myself, my career, and my ego?

▸ How can I identify the values in others? To be influential means helping others claim and honor their own personal belief system.

▸ How am I living consistent with my values? What behaviors, choices, relationships, and statements do I offer to let others know what I stand for and believe?

▸ Can I begin to see that sharing my values with others builds trust and credibility—which are paramount to being able to generate long-term influence?

Credibility is a personal asset that we must earn and then hold on to. Never risk jeopardizing your credibility by suddenly departing from your value set, hoping no one will see. Trust me: these days, everyone will see.

IN A NUTSHELL: Having the courage to *be real* and the awareness to *be credible* is how you uncover your why. The essence, root, and foundation of all you'll do in your influence journey starts here. There are no shortcuts, and you can't fake it. Breathe into who you are, why you're here, and how you'll serve. What you'll find will be more amazing than you can imagine!

CHAPTER 3

Find Your Who

> ## Who...
>
> **Be of Service**
> to have lasting
> impact.
>
> **Be Inclusive**
> of others wherever
> and however they
> are.

THE BIG IDEA: Connect with those you want to serve while remaining open to others. While you might focus your efforts on one specific group, there may be others who are interested or will benefit from what you offer, so stay curious. Today you must find your people at all stations of the company, organization, community, and world, and lead them as they need and as you're designed.

Has this ever happened to you?

You go through your schooling and take all the required courses, choose a major that's "parent approved," and set out to start a career. You take an entry-level job; get promoted; endure a few layoffs, job changes, and promotions; and keep moving forward as the hamster wheel of your career turns in predictable clockwise direction. You look around you at the people you spend your day with and realize that you all are marching in the same direction, fulfilling similar expectations, and advancing in your jobs right on schedule. Day after day. Rinse and repeat.

Then the nagging questions begin to wake you at night: *What if I'm meant to do more? What if what I'm doing and the people I'm doing it with aren't right for me?* You wonder what life would look like with more clarity, purpose, and intention . . . and different people.

You may not have a sense of who you're supposed to serve and help and guide and influence. I sure didn't. In my entire professional career, I'd never had a crystal-clear view of where I was going, who I'd work for or with, and what I wanted as reward.

For years I blindly followed the path that seemed most obvious and acceptable. I achieved the tasks and goals set by my job description; helped people just starting out; learned some skills; and, each time I changed jobs, increased my salary. I thought this was what it meant to be successful. My turning point came in 2008, when the US economy collapsed, people all around me were being laid off and losing their (heavily mortgaged) homes, and news headlines seemed like an episode of the *Twilight Zone*. Things were scary!

Amidst all the turmoil and stress, and with two kids about to head off to college, I did something I'd never done before: I took a step back. After being laid off from a fancy high-profile job, I wrote a job description for what I'd love to do. I reflected on the parts of each job I'd had over the years and what I loved to do, who I loved to work with, and how I loved to be. What brought me the most fulfillment, the most joy, and the greatest personal rewards? As I wrote out this job description and matched it with my résumé, success was written all over it! The problem was that this ideal job didn't exist. I'd have to create it.

In that moment, twenty years into my "successful" career, I gambled on entrepreneurship. I took a chance on myself. I truly believed I was meant for something more, something more colorful and expressive and authentic and hard and fun. And I knew I'd need to think, act, and show up differently to make that happen. What worked in the past would not work in this new venture. So, I reached down into my soul, and I learned to trust myself, my process, my gut, and my faith to guide me. Risky? Sure. Paid off? Big time!

I'm not advocating that you abandon the advice of your executive coach, accountability partner, rabbi, boss, or mentor, but if you can get comfortable trusting your gut and your heart and thinking about your future in terms of ideal direction rather than ideal job description, I'm your kind of people.

When I started my company in 2008, I knew I'd want to continue to serve others, in addition to generating revenue. I had always enjoyed being involved in my community during my twenty-year tenure in Corporate America, and I didn't want to lose that sense of serving as a business owner. That was all the direction I needed. I didn't have a clear picture of who I'd serve or how, and I didn't set aside a specific number of hours a week to serve. I just created space in my head and my heart and my business for service and knew it would find me.

Fast-forward a year to November 2009. At a Denver Broncos football game, I learned of the challenge faced by many US veterans leaving military service: How do they tell their story, relate to civilian counterparts, and position themselves to find meaning and influence after military duty? Not having any knowledge or personal connection to the military at the time didn't stop me. The idea was planted, the door had been opened, and I walked through it. (To learn more about my discovery process and learning, check out my TEDx Talk "The Power of Gratitude and Generosity: Serving Those Who've Served" on YouTube.)

And here's why these next two rules matter so much: We live in a world where many people are selfish, self-absorbed, and concerned only about doing that which directly benefits them. A world where kids were raised to believe they could do anything and be anything ("here's your trophy"), and often that didn't include serving others. We put up walls, lock our doors, and gate our communities to keep others out, yet we post on social media about our lavish meals and opulent homes to flaunt our good fortune (#blessed). True and lasting influence doesn't come from getting and accumulating, it comes from giving and serving.

Identifying Your Who

It's time to find your people, your tribe, your community. Your people are the ones who need you, who need to be represented and led by you. They're craving what you have to offer, like a child chasing the ice cream truck on a hot summer day—they desperately need you and want you! I saw the military community as one that met my need to serve others: they are committed to a purpose bigger than themselves (the mission), they operate in a brotherhood/sisterhood that drives unwavering loyalty and support for each other, and they need what I have to offer (tools, insights, resources, and steps to find their next path).

Once you identify your people, the ones you'll serve with passion, trust, and authenticity, be sure you're well versed on the issues they care about. Just because you see a need doesn't mean you're the right person to solve that need. I desperately worried about this point when I started investing my time and talents to serve them: Would my lack of understanding of the military experience, lingo, and acronyms be a deterrent? Like me, you'll need to invest time, energy, and heart into learning and caring about these people. You'll listen more than you speak, ask the questions that get past the surface answers, and apply what you know and who you are to serving them. They can likely tell if your efforts are self-serving and you're helping them for personal gain or if you truly want to lift them up.

Have the tough conversations, ask the right questions, and then just listen. Listen to how they share, what they say, and what they don't say. Do they trust you enough to be vulnerable and raw with you? If not, keep nurturing, building trust, and caring about them until they do.

Actions matter to those we serve. It's not enough to tell someone to follow you and know you have their back. You'll need to show them, over and over. Risk your own sense of dignity and safety to be visible and curious and real with the people you'll serve. They're not expecting you to be perfect, but they are counting on you to *be real*, in what you say and how you behave.

The first time I was given the opportunity to teach a program on military transition (through the lens of personal branding, which I know very well), I walked into the room with the confidence of Walter White in a cartel standoff (gratuitous *Breaking Bad* reference here . . .). I had my presentation on a thumb drive, my clicker (slide advancer) was fully charged, and I was dressed to be respectful to this group of Army Rangers, Navy SEALs, Green Berets, and Top Gun pilots who were making the move from elite military duty to civilian career. I thought I had the answers they wanted—and I quickly realized I would fall short.

There was still so much I didn't know. I'd never spent time in the military, so my understanding of their needs and fears and goals was limited. I knew my topic, but I needed to learn more from them. Throughout the three-hour workshop, instead of me talking at them, we discussed the ideas and resources I was presenting to them. They shared what it felt like for them to hear my suggestions, they talked of their dreams and hopes, and I shared my deep appreciation for all they'd done to ensure my safety and freedom as an American. By the end of the program, I had earned their trust and shared helpful tools. Even today, I stay in touch with many of those brave men and women from that first workshop. Online and in person, they began to tell others who were leaving the military about me and my offer. We built a community of our own.

Again, we can't thrust data, ideas, or tools at someone and assume they'll adopt them even if those are, in fact, exactly what they need. And we certainly can't believe that they'll want what we have to offer just because we're good at what we do. They need to want to believe us, trust us, and be influenced by us for us to make a lasting and meaningful impact.

If you speak over their heads, they'll tune you out. Like Charlie Brown's classroom teacher, all they'll hear is "wanh, wanh, wanh" as you try to align your mission and vision with theirs. Similarly, address them with too much familiarity, they could become skeptical: *Who is this person who claims to know what I feel and need? They're not like me!* Act too raw, exposed, and vulnerable, and they might question your competence: *Please do not tell the story of your complicated divorce again, Susan. . . .* Your people have specific needs and feelings and goals and dreams and fears, and your job is to know them intimately and respond accordingly.

Note: It's not feasible to help everyone, everywhere. Sure, it would be super-fantastic-awesome if we could help, heal, motivate, impact, grow, and serve every human on the planet with our goodness. But it's not realistic.

Instead, focus on the people and communities who need you the most, so you can see and feel your influence grow.

Before you feel bad that there are some people you won't be able to reach and serve, know that there will be a ripple effect to your impact. You'll empower, teach, and inspire people to go and continue your vision in new communities, with new beneficiaries and groups, and that's the beauty of all this! But you must get the ball started, to know who your people are and what they need to know and feel from you.

Personas

In marketing, we draw personas to capture the characteristics, personality traits, and needs of our target audience. When promoting or marketing a product or service to a persona, we need to know how that person buys, what turns them off, and what turns them on. While we should be careful not to overgeneralize, we must get inside their head to think like them so that we can shop or buy like them.

Similarly, draw out personas for your people: Where are they? How do they gather (online? in person? in open forums or private rooms?), who do they trust, and who inspires them? What keeps them up at night, and what do they dream about when they sleep? With that information, paint a picture of who they are, even assigning them names to identify them in your own mind. You might have a persona for your boss, your colleagues, your mentees, and your support network. This helps you speak to them in the tone, tenor, volume, and language they'll relate to and understand.

Get clear on how much they know about your topic or cause. If there's a steep learning curve, for example, who will you enlist to help you? What media or influencers do these people pay attention to? How do you compare to those outlets in message and delivery?

Again, I'll use my example of the military community here. To understand them, I embedded myself into their world through discussion, mentoring, and reading. I then drew personas around who I'd help as they navigated the military-to-civilian transition.

I drew a persona around Person A, the person who's exiting the military with confidence, clarity, and a sense of direction. They had a great support network and education and focused on building their network of contacts at the same time they served our country. I learned what they cared about, who they took advice from, and the kind of work they'd pursue. They had no idea of personal branding.

I drew a persona for Person B, the younger soldier or airman or sailor who didn't know what they didn't know. They may have worked a desk job or a trade (such as a mechanic) and lacked exposure to career ideas and options that could work for them. They worried whether leaving the military was a smart move (too much risk) but weren't happy being in uniform. They needed more skills, education, and tools to navigate civilian reintegration, but had no idea where to start. They'd never heard of personal branding.

And there was Person C, the individual leaving the military with some ideas—some vision for what could come next—but who needed help translating their past into their future. They may or may not have heard of personal branding, but they were open to the ideas I'd present, and to applying themselves in new ways to find happiness after exiting the military.

As you clarify your "who," clarify their needs, values, and passions. You might draw personas like:

▶ Children born with a physical disability, who're limited in their movement and abilities to thrive. Whether in underserved populations or urban communities, these children are missing out on life's joy because they can't access resources.

These children want to be "normal" and not looked at for their difference. Their parents want to give their child the opportunity to be a kid. There are barriers keeping this from happening, which I am committed to change.

▶ Young Hispanic girls in inner-city Chicago, Los Angeles, New York, and Miami who seek role models in fashion but don't have access to the internet, magazines, or people who can show them what that looks like.

They care about pretty clothes, well-fitting garments, confidence, a career and life beyond the neighborhood, helping their families, and being independent.

▶ My team. They work so hard for this company and have weathered many storms with me and the company as we've navigated mergers and downturns. Today, they are worried about their futures, careers, and ability to provide for their families.

They look to me to advocate for them—to be their champion and stand up for them. I will use my voice, influence, and experience to be their advocate with senior management and across the industry.

▶ Military veterans. They care about mission and service and want to know that their work in the private sector can still have meaning.

They want to continue to provide for their loved ones and seek to expand their influence in the world. They may have residual traumas to wrestle with and limitations because of invisible challenges, and they navigate those with a servant's heart, resolute loyalty and commitment, and a desire to leave the world a better place than they found it.

▶ Immigrant families who face barriers in language, education, and resources to start a new life in the United States. Regardless of their status, they are struggling to stay safe, sheltered, and fed.

They want to embrace the American dream—to work, provide for their children, and send money home to relatives. They care about quality of life, maintaining their cultural roots, and navigating the legal, social, and political system in the US to be productive and happy families. They are marginalized by current systems.

The People You'll Influence Aren't Linear

When considering who you'll influence, remember that you may need to influence up, down, and across. You may find the most impact from influencing your boss's boss, the media outlets your constituents read, or stakeholders who are further removed than you originally believed. To sell your vision, consider your primary audience (who'll make the ultimate decision to support you) and then secondary audiences (the more tangential audiences who'll also need to adopt and believe in your vision and story to help promote and accept your vision).

I remember early in my career trying to get the attention of a prospective client who had more gatekeepers in place than the pope. Layer after layer of people telling me no was frustrating and exciting at the same time (it certainly triggered my competitive side!). One day, as I made my five millionth call to this person's office to try to speak with him, his administrative assistant asked me, "Why do you keep calling? What are you trying to tell him that's so important?"

What a great question! I shared with her how strongly I believed in the services I was selling as a business development agent. I truly saw lives changed and people's businesses improved, and that meant so much to me. I told her the story of how I got into the business and why perseverance was part of my commitment to serve my clients. I then asked her why she felt strongly about the work she was doing.

She told me about her first years at the company, and how she fell in love with their products and the people who made them. Her boss oversaw the corporate vision, and that meant she was connected to something bigger.

The conversation continued and slowly I could feel our symbiotic energies connect. We felt equally passionate about what we were doing, and that meant she was more inclined to help me. Why hadn't I thought of that earlier?! She was a secondary audience—her boss made the ultimate decision to say yes, but she was the reason I got a call through to him. Consider who's influencing the people you're trying to reach with your message. Who has their trust and attention? As you promote your vision, these people are very important!

RULE 4: BE OF SERVICE to Have Lasting Impact

Working alongside service members, veterans, and military families for so many years, I've learned about their unwavering commitment to the act of service. As we have an all-volunteer military in the US, these men and women raised their hand to defend and possibly die for the freedom and liberties I, and others like me, enjoy. When they serve, they protect those around them with their own lives ("I've got your six"). Even after military duty, that sense of service doesn't leave them. They're the employees who will gladly help others, even if it doesn't benefit them and their position. They're the entrepreneur who wants to prevent others from committing suicide after military separation and invests their life savings into a technology solution. They end their calls with, "How can I help you?"

As statistics show, most of us in the US haven't served in the military. But we can still serve to have lasting impact. First you'll need to decide who you'll serve. The how and when come later.

Answer these questions:

- ► What if someone needs what you offer, but they can't pay you? Will you find a workaround and still help them?

- ► Can you work with people who aren't fully vested in the idea or who can challenge you at every step?

- ► Are you most committed to serving people who've had a specific experience (e.g., been homeless, been held back in their career, lost venture funding, been the target of hate, lost a baby, or otherwise directly endured what you're seeking to change)?

- ► Can you serve people who are vastly different from yourself?

- ► If you want to serve people who don't share your background, how will you learn about their issues, concerns, and challenges?

My friend Ali leveraged her superior creative writing skills to write the little descriptions the animal shelter lists for each pet, hoping to attract adoptive parents. My colleague Chris, a professional recruiter, volunteers his time on the weekends to mentor job seekers through a local nonprofit. He offers tips, insights, and advice and is not trying to solicit their business. There are people all around us knitting beanies for premature babies in the NICU, working in the synagogue's soup kitchen, teaching immigrants to navigate city resources, and so on. We can find acts of service everywhere!

Service Is Both a Mindset and an Action

You must believe in service to truly serve. Being "of service" is not just about writing donation checks or lending your name to rubber-chicken fundraising banquets for a local nonprofit. Sure, ask any nonprofit organization if they appreciate donations and they'll utter a resounding, "Heck, yeah!" but they also need people to roll up their sleeves and get work done.

I remember working with Alan (not his real name), a prominent scientist in the field of gene therapy. Alan was revered, awarded, celebrated, and fawned over wherever he went. He was the Tom Brady of science, as he liked to refer to himself. If you follow football or sports, you know Brady. If you know science, you know Alan.

He also considered himself to be a very generous, service-focused individual. When I worked with him on his personal brand and influence strategy, he wanted to articulate and leverage his "servant leader" brand. I asked him to clarify what service meant to him. He explained, "It's giving to someone else when they need help or advice. If I can offer it, I do. When someone needs me, it means I'll be there." Okay, I'm tracking with you, Alan.

Then came the hard part.

I asked him to share a few examples of times he's been of service, whom he served, and what the conditions were. He first told me about a young research fellow who'd joined his team. This person reported to Alan and was nervous about being in his presence. This flattered Alan, so he spent extra time explaining things and introducing him to others who could help his career. This was his service.

There was the community organization that was giving him an honorary award and asked him to come speak, and in turn Alan waived his traditional speaking fee to show his support of their work. This was also his service.

The more we talked, the more I learned that while he intended to have a servant's heart, he did so where it served him most. The young research fellow flattered Alan and thus received job perks. The organization honored Alan, so he gave a presentation for free. Is that how we define service?

I asked Alan if he'd consider doing those things anonymously or without attribution or credit. This did not sit well with him. "How am I building influence if I don't get credit?" he asked. To Alan, if the tree fell in the forest and no one was there to capture it for Instagram (tagging him, of course), it didn't fall. And therein lies the issue: service lives in your heart, not on your résumé.

Alan believed he could outsource his service and build influence by strategically aligning his name and presence where it benefited him. He sought opportunities where the profit margins were highest (not of the greatest value to beneficiaries), sought credit and recognition for what he gave ("is someone filming this?"), and wasn't willing to put skin in the game and take the risks to serve. He couldn't imagine being laughed at, coming across as unknowing, or exposing his vulnerabilities to learn and embrace what his audience needed from him. In the end, Alan remained scripted, polished, rehearsed . . . and ineffective.

When someone has service in their heart, it oozes from them. They can't help it. They hear a story on the news, and they want to help. Someone on the team is struggling, and they reach out to assist even if it's not their job to do so. They learn of a community that's struggling, and they pull together their resources (friends, contacts, money, etc.) to help the people in need. Service is a non-negotiable quality of how they live their lives.

How to Be of Service

"I don't have time."

"It sounds too hard."

"I don't know where to start."

Sound familiar? Yes, we're all running super busy lives with massive to-do lists that must be checked off at warp speed, or the planet will fall off its axis (or so it seems). The truth is, there's always time to serve others, too.

There are many ways to serve, and when we add service into the context of influence, we immediately see that service is about the people, communities, constituents, and customers you seek to drive change with, not about what you can get out of them. When we serve with a pure heart, we build dignity in others. We lift them up, and in turn they're inspired to do the same for others. Service is not finite or peripheral, it's fluid and moving and ongoing—it's "pay it forward."

A client of mine once described their favorite boss to me. He talked about this boss's technical acumen and his experience in the company and industry. "But what made him my favorite boss is how he showed up: each time there was a contentious meeting—say, between the customer, our tech team, and our service team—this boss always asked, 'How can I help?' There was never hesitation. He didn't wait to see which side was right or wrong or which angle afforded him the best exposure. He showed such courage and resolve, but he also showed service to each of the individuals who needed to feel heard."

My client shared how this boss used validation as a skill to be sure he never interrupted when someone shared an idea or a concern. He acknowledged that he'd heard them and validated that their solution or complaint had merit. He didn't agree on all counts, but because he was service oriented, he made sure there were solutions on the table that made everyone feel whole.

When you're serving them, the focus is on them, not you.

A few years into my professional speaking work, I had done a lot of presentations for a local school district. I loved the opportunity to share personal branding and reputation management techniques with superintendents, school administrators, and other district leaders. One day, I was asked to present a personal branding program to their school bus drivers as part of a multiday intensive on "future-proofing their careers." *Yes! This is my wheelhouse!*

With all the enthusiasm of a puppy in a tennis ball factory, I walked onstage, clicker in hand, and began talking through my presentation. I had inflection in my voice and passion in my words; my program, as great as I knew it was, would surely dazzle them into knowing how to grow their careers.

About fifteen minutes in, I looked out into the room and saw every speaker's nightmare: the audience was checked out. Their arms were crossed, their heads were shaking, and some were whispering to their neighbors—and I knew it wasn't to share something positive about what they were hearing.

Flag on the play!

I drew in a deep breath, put the clicker on the lectern, and took a step forward to my audience. I abandoned the presentation and told them, from my heart, what it felt like as a parent to put my two school-age children on their bus each morning, hoping to God the driver was sober, awake, and aware of the precious cargo they carried.

I told them of the respect parents have (or should have) for their role—how vital a part of each child's education they were. Without them, our lives could have been negatively impacted.

Because I'd been able to read the room and remember that my role was not to share my vision and message with myself, but with them, and to help them become more confident, empowered, and fulfilled, I could pivot. Their crossed arms slowly unfolded, they sat up in their seats, heads began nodding in agreement, and they finally saw me—not as a professional speaker delivering a canned message, but as a parent who valued them and wanted to serve them.

They also gave me my first-ever standing ovation.

Think about the Long Game

When we serve others, and it's not for our own benefit or agenda, we do so as an investment. We're investing in someone's life, career, position, place in the world. We're pouring out goodness while knowing we may never see how it turns out—how they take that goodness and make the world a better place. This trust and faith are where true influential leaders find patience. They're not striving for immediate results and seeking credit for their effort. They're investing in others' lives because it's the right thing to do. The moral/Christian/humanity-focused thing to do—their values direct their actions toward helping others, maybe because they themselves were helped.

Mentoring is a great technique to show service to others. I've had the honor to mentor several women as I climbed the corporate ladder in my career. Their questions, challenges, and ideas were inspiring to me, as I was several rungs ahead of them. I've also had the privilege of mentoring hundreds of active-duty service members, military spouses, and veterans. Their questions, challenges, and ideas might be vastly different, but knowing that what I've learned in my life and career could be of service to someone else navigating *their* life and career gives me perspective.

Being of service and investing in others empowers us to see the frailty of our time on Earth, the quick pace at which wrinkles appear, gray hairs sprout, and our step slows. We begin to see our own lives as if we're far out in space, looking back on the planet and realizing how small we truly are on that blue dot over there, our home country.

The smallness of our own lives is made bigger and more significant when we give to others, when we serve. It's then that our learnings, struggles, traumas, gifts, and talents live on through others. Organ donors sometimes describe the feeling they have when they know their body parts will be helping someone else live a more fulfilling and longer life; it's as if they'll also live on. That's how it is to influence with a service mindset.

Service for you might look like:

- ► Mentoring someone who could learn from your experience, but where there's no financial gain for yourself.

- ► Being positive and uplifting to keep your team engaged and happy.

- ► Rolling up your sleeves and volunteering in a soup kitchen, at-risk youth center, women's shelter, or veterans' group home.

- ► Letting someone else on the team offer a great idea first, building on it later, so they get credit.

- ► Sitting with someone going through a tough time. Not offering advice or guidance or suggestions—just being present with them.

- ► Volunteering to work with kids on the autism spectrum who're struggling with social skills.

- ► Coaching your team to be better, stronger, faster, and cleverer so they'll advance past you.

- ► Putting someone on your team up for a promotion to a great position in another department because it's what they want.

- ► Helping without seeking credit, recognition, or praise (the military calls this "service before self").

- ► Caring or assisting someone when it's not in your job description.

- ► Using your voice to amplify a community that's powerless to advocate for themselves.

Service Is Multidimensional

Influence isn't coercion (telling others what to do) or compliance ("I'll follow your vision because it's in my job description"). We can tell when someone's helping us or leading us from their motives or our own. As influence is the way we inspire, impact, and guide people toward an idea, belief, suggestion, or vision, we must be of service to them for the influence to be meaningful, scalable, and sustainable.

A service mindset also means you plan for your influence to grow beyond you. There's a wonderful little book I read many years ago that shaped my thinking on this idea. In this book, *The Cathedral Within*, author and social entrepreneur Bill Shore lays out the importance of vision setting, as demonstrated by the original architects of ancient cathedrals. The book contains numerous stories of social influencers whose vision is so clear, measurable, and service-based that it endures well beyond the life of its originator. Much like cathedrals of long ago, the structures, systems, and ideas sought to serve a mission and purpose that mattered, and thus have been transferred and adopted by modern beneficiaries.

Influence also requires you to empower the people you serve to take your mission and vision further than you possibly can. This means you'll have to get comfortable sharing credit, embracing collective thought and momentum, and seeking the greater good (not followers, awards, or promotions).

Questions to ask yourself:

▶ When am I of service to others? How do I know—am I mindful of my intentions?

- What feelings does my service give me? It's okay to get satisfaction, joy, or pride from serving.
- What is the impact of my service? Can I see others thriving or being inspired because of my influence?
- Who am I most passionate about serving? Who am I least passionate about serving?

As you grow into your service to others, check in with yourself: Are you seeking credit and adding the service to your résumé and LinkedIn profile? Is that diminishing the value of your service, or allowing you to tell more people about the great work you're doing and hopefully leading them to do the same? Only you can know for sure.

RULE 5: BE INCLUSIVE of Others Wherever and However They Are

Okay, before you shoot the messenger and think this is yet another HR-mandated message telling us all to get along, let's define inclusivity.

Inclusivity has gotten a bad rap from some, as it feels like a mandated "everyone plays nice in the sandbox" message. We're taught not to see color and not to consider age, gender, religion, or background when considering our peers and how we'll speak to or treat them. But that, we know, is unrealistic. Like many of you, I want people to see my physical attributes and my heritage and what I've done to earn my spot. I want to be regarded as a successful female entrepreneur not because I'm a female, but because of who I am—and being female is partly how

I define myself. I'm proud of my family's well-known heritage and history, the differences I represent that make me unique in my industry, and the sameness that connects me to my fellow human beings. Inclusivity, as I define it, sees all of who we are and celebrates it!

I'm certainly not minimizing the plight and efforts of groups who've been marginalized or felt slighted. As a woman in business, at times I definitely felt my gender get in the way of promotion or advancement because of misconceptions about how I might be in that role (Will she cry in a meeting? Is she planning to have more kids?), whereas my male counterparts didn't encounter those obstacles. I know I was fortunate to advance to my station in part because of advantages I had that others didn't. I don't apologize for how I got here. I embrace it. I'm grateful for it all. And similar advantages presented an "easy road" for some of my peers who don't possess one-tenth of the resiliency and tenacity as my less fortunate counterparts who've surpassed us because of their drive, commitment, and grit.

Being inclusive builds influence because you're choosing to be open; willing to hear different viewpoints; and considering alternative ways, ideas, and visions. Inclusivity means deciding who needs to be in the room, then *seeing* everyone in the room and making it a priority that they feel seen and heard. When people around you feel safe, heard, and understood for who they are, where they are, and what they can offer, you've built an inclusive environment. When we are truly inclusive, we create *psychological safety* for those around us—a concept explored in the great work of Amy Edmondson, the Harvard

Business School professor who coined the term. When people feel safe, they'll share their concerns and ideas and take risks because they feel supported. Inclusivity is very much a mindset and choice, not something you learn in a training manual with a quiz at the end. Inclusivity dictates that when we serve and seek to influence others, we must do so with a curious mind and heart, not a judgmental or protective one. This can be scary. Being open can feel like you're receptive to having your beliefs, cultural norms, upbringing, values, faith, and principles challenged and even changed. And in part, that's the point. If your views are based on limited or incorrect input or learning, I encourage you to consider how far your influence will take you if you're not open to change. If you were raised or surrounded yourself with people with a limiting mindset, you will undoubtedly see limits, threats, and hurt around you (later I'll discuss the *Tetris* effect to illustrate this point), and this won't serve you or anyone else.

We can't possibly know what someone else is going through—even the best mind reader acts in Las Vegas can't—so we can't assume we understand someone's situation. "They're looking for a shortcut," "He wants to hold me back," and "She's lazy," are toxic assumptions we can make that serve no one, particularly you, as you grow your voice and value to the world around you.

You can see color and embrace it or choose to be limited by it. You can seek to hear from the marginalized or less educated voices in the room, who are often overlooked, or ignore them as others have. Being inclusive means you bring everyone to the table to participate in shaping the vision, creating the plan, and ideating what could be.

The flip side to this is surrounding yourself only with people who think like you and agree with you. Yes, this might feel like a more comfortable scenario, where you offer an idea or initiative and the bobbleheads in the room fervently nod in agreement, leading you to believe in your own brilliance. But are you considering all viewpoints? Have you stretched outside of what's comfortable and known and "normal" to look at your idea from all angles?

For you, inclusivity might look like:

▶ Refraining from starting a conversation or meeting with "Hey, guys!" so everyone (including your female and nonbinary colleagues) feels seen and recognized.

▶ Seeking out differing viewpoints to challenge your assumptions and beliefs. This could mean watching alternative news outlets, reading different publications, or hosting conversations on controversial topics with industry or community leaders—all to gather a well-rounded perspective.

▶ Surrounding yourself with people from different backgrounds, lifestyles, and cultures to enhance your view of the world. If you bring an open, growth mindset to the conversation, you'll find your perspective expanding, not shrinking.

▶ Allowing yourself to be comfortable getting uncomfortable. Let yourself consider another viewpoint even if on the surface it feels like it could clash with your values. There's no harm in listening and considering.

Include different thoughts and ideas and perspectives and backgrounds to get the fullest picture. Let those ideas and thoughts push you further than you think you can go and shape your vision in diverse and more equitable ways. Remember, this isn't a zero-sum game! When you open your heart and mind, no one is losing here. You're still in control of what you think and feel.

We've all heard that hurt people hurt people. I also believe people who love and give their light to others receive love and light in return. If you're not willing to be inclusive and of service and to share with others, how can you expect others to want to be of service and include you?

My client Ahmad practices an inclusive mindset in his work. The leader of a large technology company, he often works across the company to solve organizational problems, introduce new products, or align groups toward a new focus. I've seen him fill a meeting with such disparate voices, faces, backgrounds, and experiences that it feels like a mini–United Nations in the room. Each person is there for a reason—they represent a viewpoint, perspective, or possible insight—and he honors each of them with patience, validation, and inclusion in the conversation. Ahmad lets everyone be part of the process: everyone has a voice; everyone is seen and heard. And then, remarkably, at the end of each meeting, he asks the group, "If there's someone who should have been in this meeting that I neglected to include, please let me know and I'll circle around to them. I want to hear from everyone." Wow!

While "inclusivity" might be the zeitgeist of the twenty-first century, to live inclusively, lead as someone committed to inclusivity, and ensure that everyone's voice is recognized and everyone is seen actually sets you apart today and into the future. Inclusivity is a mindset, a commitment, an umbrella under which we all fit beautifully. It's also a key element in influence.

Questions to ask yourself:

► When I must decide, do I consider other viewpoints besides my own?

► If I'm challenged on an idea, could they be pointing out a blind spot or my ignorance on an issue?

► How can I work more inclusive conversations into my workday?

► Do I make others feel safe sharing their ideas and views with me?

► When I think about how I'll influence others, could there be tangential groups also impacted or affected? Have I considered their views?

Inclusivity is not an end state. You don't check enough boxes and then get a gold star that says, "Congratulations, you're inclusive!" It's a process by which you open your mind and heart to others. Along with a service mindset and a commitment to take the time to consider all voices, being inclusive can be the most loving, giving, and impactful part of building influence.

IN A NUTSHELL: When we focus in on who we want to influence, it might feel like we're taking the "art" of influence away and making it more strategic, operational, and clinical. Maybe we are. The world is way too busy and loud and competitive to just believe if you stand on the steps of the Lincoln Memorial in Washington, DC, and preach your message, others will follow you. Today, to get the attention and hearts of the people you want to serve and influence, you need to be strategic and inclusive about who they are and what they need from you.

CHAPTER 4

Clarify Your *How*

How...

Be Consistent
in who and how
you are.

Be Agile
to learn and grow.

Be a Storyteller
to share your why.

THE BIG IDEA: To have influence means taking action, balancing consistency with agility, and being open to learning and adapting based on new information and points of view. Then, you'll share your vision and mission with others by telling your story and articulating your "why" so they can align.

Is your goal for building influence so you can lead others? It's a real question. Not everyone wants to lead—many are happy taking a support role but still want to have their voice, opinions, and value matter.

If you do want to lead others, you'll need to inspire and motivate people to follow you. There are thousands of available leadership training programs, but unless you truly feel in your gut that leading is your calling—the only option—and you're willing to lead with your whole heart, soul, and body, you may not succeed at it.

Both leadership and influence require you to deploy imagination and creativity. Not the kind where you make up stories, data, and relationships to advance your position, but the kind you'll use to share your vision, reach your people, and develop your influence over time.

I believe that imagination is highly underrated. So often we value results, metrics and outcomes, and the information and numbers that support success. But what about the ideation that it took to get there, the creative trials and errors that tested someone so much they almost quit (but didn't)? Imagination is what military leaders need to deploy on the battlefield when the best-laid plan goes wrong. It's what brings us inventors and entrepreneurs and visionaries who change the world because they ask, "What if . . .?" and "Why couldn't we . . .?" instead of accepting how things are and have always been. Imagination, combined with courage and credibility, drives change and often changes the status quo.

Get Going with Your How

Working the Rules in a harmonious way takes practice. At first it might feel like learning to dance the tango: one foot goes here, then this foot moves there, then the first foot comes back—and work the arms! Don't forget the arms....

To promote your vision to others, you'll need to be clear about it and organize your thoughts such that telling a story or building your credibility feels seamless. To do this, it helps to break your big vision down into smaller goals.

Think of your vision this way:

- ▸ **What is the problem you're solving or the improvement you're offering?** Use layperson's terms to explain what it is your vision will achieve, change, help, or address. Be as specific as possible.

- ▸ **Who will benefit from having this problem solved or this improvement offered?** Here, consider primary and secondary audiences (personas) who'll be served by your vision.

- ▸ **What will be the measurable impact of your vision?** How will someone's life be improved? What difference will they be able to make in the world with this barrier removed? Think past the immediate benefits of having an issue resolved to the long-term impact to the individual, community, society, or the planet.

Your mission might not be world-changing, big, or ambitious, and that's okay. Maybe you're looking to influence conversations more confidently in your work or industry. Perhaps you seek to make a positive impression when you speak up in a company meeting. Or perhaps you're going to write a book or speak on a topic of great importance to your community. Whatever level of influence you seek to assert, the formula still works: *know your why, focus on your who, and get going with your how.*

RULE 6: BE CONSISTENT in Who and How You Are

Building influence doesn't require perfection, but it does require consistency. Being the same person online as in the flesh, representing values that you promote over time, and aligning your actions with core principles gives others the assurance to trust (and follow) your vision.

Consistency still means being able to mix up your wardrobe, your friend groups, and your social media profile pictures, but across all touchpoints, your audience should believe they're seeing, learning from, hearing, and being influenced by the same person.

If you know me, you know I've struggled with consistency. Maybe it's the Gemini in me, but I like to mix things up; to show different sides of myself; to change my website font, my hairstyle, and my profile pictures. To influence others, I had to learn to own a voice and build equity in my online profiles to help followers know that the Lida they see on LinkedIn is the same one they'll see on my website, YouTube, Instagram, and so on. Consistency builds trust.

When I change my hairstyle, I get new photos taken and switch my images out. I want my audiences to know that the person they see in front of them on stage is the same person whose LinkedIn account they're viewing from their cellphones as I speak. When my body shape changes (read: holiday pounds stay put), I get some new clothes to make sure my wardrobe fits well and is appropriate for my body. When my confidence grows, I share more personal stories of who I am, how I got here, and where I've succeeded and failed.

Consistency and Accountability

Everything I share, post, promote, or offer up is done through the lens of "Is this consistent with who I am, how I want to be known, and what I stand for?" If there's a disconnect, it needs to be fixed. Now.

I've empowered my team to help hold me accountable to this consistency. If I record a video, craft a social media post, or want to introduce a new speaking topic, they are comfortable questioning my motives (is it because that topic is trendy and I'm trying to ride the wave?), my intentions (do I see this as a way to serve or just make money?), and my voice (is this really the time to start using expletives? I just don't speak that way). While I am a good judge of my own brand and consistency goals, even I can get tempted by a hot news topic or funny joke or a bright and shiny object. Those are the mistakes that can destroy influence.

Consistency for you might mean:

▸ Keeping the same profile picture across all your social media.

▸ Speaking with the same honesty and passion whether you're at work, with friends, or at home.

▸ Finding opportunities to share who you are (as a person) with colleagues who might know you more by your job and title, rather than your background.

▸ Acting the same way whether or not you think someone is watching.

My client Greg struggles with consistency, particularly as he rebuilds his voice at work. He was raised by a strong, successful, and very "alpha" father who instilled in him that the loudest voice in the room gets the attention (he failed to explain that the attention wasn't always positive . . .). He raised Greg to believe that being a person of influence meant taking command, managing his stature and status against that of others in the room, and driving authority and power in all he did. Greg then began his career as a trial lawyer working under the mentorship of a strong, successful, and very "alpha" senior partner who also seemed to revel in adjusting Greg's style and personality.

Greg acted the part he'd been coached to assume: He stomped into depositions and stormed out of conversations he didn't like. He dismissed people around him and would intentionally call a female coworker "honey" just to undermine her confidence. These were traits even Greg recognized were counterproductive to how he wanted to be perceived and hurtful to conversations he wanted to influence.

When asked, Greg considered his true nature to be more open, approachable, and welcoming, but these two strong role models had spent years imparting a very different script into his narrative. As Greg and I worked to separate his traits and goals from those he'd been taught, which were unhealthy to him, consistency was a challenge. Greg found it more comfortable to speak as he believed was real to him and to treat others the way his heart told him was best. But slipping back into old patterns of what he'd been taught, to separate the "shoulds" from his communication and presence, was a challenge. Greg is a smart guy and a fine lawyer, but being his real self consistently at work and in the courtroom was an ongoing struggle.

We developed cues and tips for him to tap into when he found himself venturing into the black hole of that alpha male persona he'd been taught. He learned to identify the triggers that put him on the slippery slope back into the defaults of what he'd learned. He used silence strategically to "catch" himself before launching into a tirade, and he issued a heartfelt apology to his female colleague for how he'd treated her. With practice, time, and the support of better mentors, he more consistently showed up as "smart, strong, and welcoming Greg" rather than the Greg no one wanted to work with.

Consistency requires self-discipline, self-awareness, and situational awareness to know how you're behaving and being received. If you're struggling with how to consistently be the version of yourself you want to project, take a moment to review Rule 2 (Be Real) and Rule 3 (Be Credible).

Questions to ask yourself:

► Do I have a clear sense of who I am, what I stand for, and how I want to be known?

► With clarity of my vision, how can I best share my voice, using different platforms and venues as they are designed but not deviating from the authenticity of my brand?

▶ Where have I been inconsistent before? Can I remedy those instances now?

▶ What are the standards I hold myself to, to ensure consistency of my voice, values, and influence?

Ask any professional athlete why consistency is important, and they'll tell you it's because repetition, over time, instills good habits, discipline, and muscle memory. In his groundbreaking book on success, *Outliers: The Story of Success*, Malcolm Gladwell unpacked studies showing that great achievement (in music, athletics, technology, etc.) takes a consistent 10,000 hours of repetitive practice and application. Consistency pays off!

Why Is Consistency So Hard?

If we know that to be great requires building muscle memory, why aren't more of us consistent?

First, it's often easier to pivot and shift when an easier system is presented. Instead of practicing the one golf swing over and over (or for 10,000 hours), we buy an apparatus that calculates the arc of our swing and adjusts it depending on the club we're using, the climate, and the terrain. Instead of practicing the speech in advance, we "wing it" and assume the adrenaline rush will compensate for our lack of preparation. Instead of meditating, going to therapy, exercising, or practicing our prayer rituals, we take a pill to ease our stress. When given an easier route, most of us will choose it.

Second, it's hard to be consistent if we lose sight of the prize. If our motivation is to please our parents, for instance, then good grades give us rewards and praise and happy Thanksgiving holidays. But if the only reason we went to college and chose Dad's alma mater was external validation, then when that wanes, our desire to apply ourselves consistently can also vanish.

Third, consistency is hard when others around you aren't as passionate about the mission and outcome as you are. When you're the only one promoting the vision or idea, it can feel like pushing that proverbial rock uphill solo. And, if you add naysayers, doubters, and adversaries to the mix, resolve and consistency can disappear as quickly as a vampire in the daylight.

Lastly, consistency is hard to maintain if your heart isn't in it. The athlete who gets up every day at 4 a.m. to run sprints—who trains in the rain, snow, and heat and through blisters, sweat, tears, and frustration—believes in the goal. They see the process as the way to get the goal. They believe with every fiber of their being that the goal is theirs to attain if they consistently work hard at it. They break the process down to the cellular level—how much water is needed to stay hydrated, which shoes will give them the most traction and support, how to afford the best coach, and what victory will feel, taste, and smell like when they get it. The 10,000 hours is a no-brainer.

Consistency requires attention, patience, and discipline to achieve. In today's "bright and shiny" world, it's so easy to be tempted, distracted, and pulled away from what's hard, what matters, and what's scary and toward what's easy, popular, and safer. Choose consistency over comfort or shortcuts to achieve your influence—there's a reason more people don't have influence. It's not easy.

RULE 7: BE AGILE to Learn and Grow

Rigidity and limiting beliefs are old-school thinking. Today, having influence requires being able to flex and adapt and stretch and grow into changing markets and conditions, to new needs or ideas, and leveraging technologies and other people to ensure your influence can thrive.

Early in my career, I had a boss whose favorite expression was, "Well, that's how we've always done it here." Have you also had that boss? They resist innovation, a growth mindset, and anything that feels like risk to them. Even if the potential or upside is huge, they'll dig their heels in like a toddler who wants their ice cream (NOW!), unyielding to ideas, possibility, incentive, or the threat of bedtime.

To be influential requires an agility mindset. The influential leaders are the ones who, in March 2020, said, "Well, now, this is different. Global pandemic? Let's figure this out . . ." and kept their eyes open as they navigated uncharted, shark-infested waters and toilet paper shortages. Change, uncertainty, disaster, threat, obstacles, and challenges are a certainty in business and society. To be influential and project confidence means riding the waves of uncertainty, planning as best as you can for positive outcomes, listening to the input of others, and mitigating risk.

One of my all-time favorite books is the classic *Who Moved My Cheese?* by Dr. Spencer Johnson. The first time I read this simplistic story of adversity, change, and the ability to flex, I marveled at how practical it was. I began giving copies to students graduating college, friends during a job loss, and colleagues stuck in their careers. It is that versatile of a read.

The book highlights four characters' struggle to find the cheese in a maze. Each character represents a common reaction to adversity: embracing change, running toward the situation, freezing, or pondering incessantly. They struggle to find the cheese, which represents a powerful and delicious metaphor for all that we want in life. Throughout the story, we see how various tactics don't work and how trying to insist they will because "they worked in the past" is outdated thinking. There are good times (we have lots of cheese) and times of scarcity (where'd the cheese go?), but it's how we respond when we're faced with the question "What would I do if I wasn't afraid?" that can move us to greatness.

Agility is about being able not only to flex and adapt, but also to act quickly. Decisiveness and mental agility are necessary. When the pandemic hit, I was coming off a crazy year—I'd run myself ragged traveling and writing a lot, coaching high-profile clients, and managing a busy home life. While the idea of a respite from work (as things shut down around me) sounded ideal, the timing was challenging.

You see, in 2019, as I was jetting off to all corners of the world to teach and promote my message, what I hadn't had time for was processing the recent death of my father, the person on this planet I was closest to. In fact, at the end of February 2020 as I returned from a business trip—where I'd spent most of the night filling out police reports when my rental car was vandalized in the hotel parking lot, and then had to present a five-hour workshop with zero sleep and lots of caffeine and adrenaline—I planned to give myself some time off. I knew I hadn't grieved my father yet and had been in autopilot mode to get through what I needed to do to keep the sails pointing in the right direction. I was planning to take part of the spring to relax, reflect, go for long walks at the lake near my home, and process losing my dad.

Instead, Covid hit. Already raw, unstable, and vulnerable from the past year, I was shaken hard by the uncertainty of what we were all facing. Really hard. I stocked up on toilet paper (didn't we all?), protein shakes (worst case, if there's no food, we can get skinny!), and all-purpose flour. I have no idea why I needed flour, but it felt like the right thing to do when nothing felt right.

As events started canceling, travel stopped, and convention halls began boarding up, I also recognized that my work as an in-person speaker would not return, at least for a long time. Having done webinars and virtual events in the past, I leaned into this. I spoke to a colleague in Texas who was an audiovisual guru and got a list of equipment I'd need to level up my programs from a tech perspective. Several microphones, lights, booms, a mixing board, and 4k camera later, I had an incredible studio in my home office. I pursued media interviews and repeatedly heard how professional and polished my setup looked. I fine-tuned my background and was ready to go into a new offer for my business: virtual programs.

I chose to delay diving deep into my grief and processing the loss of my father to ensure my business would survive. Grief could wait a little bit longer.* I began booking many web-based programs and keynote speeches. Companies around the world began to offer my programs to their global audiences, who previously would've had to travel to a meeting location (at considerable expense) but now could enjoy the offerings from the comfort of their kitchen tables. The speaking model had shifted, and I was ahead of the curve to ride the wave. In fact, in 2021, as things were still mostly virtual, I had one of my most profitable years as LIDA360.

For you, being agile might mean:

▸ Spending money when you're worried about income.

▸ Working from your home office when you prefer to be on stage.

▸ Hiring when everyone else is laying off. In 2020, I also hired my Marketing Manager, who's still with me today. I needed to beef up visibility to get the word out about my offer—and how my clients could still get the goodness I could deliver but do it virtually. The investment in a person (whose family

---

* Grief, I learned, is a process, not an event. You don't "get over" losing someone, you just get through it, and I still am. Dr. Seuss's words really helped me, and may resonate with you if you're facing loss: "Don't be sad because it's over. Smile because it happened."

would depend on the income) was also terrifying.
Agility requires Courage (Rule #1).

▸ Taking a step backwards to evaluate the landscape
  ahead.

▸ Resisting the urge to be angry about your circumstances and instead ask "what's possible?"

Emotional Agility

Most often when I use the word *agility*, people think of
Agile, the project management system, or physical agility—being able to run, jump, and climb trees. In fact,
like physical agility, being able to project confidence and
impact others requires keeping your muscles toned, loose,
and stretched.

Emotional agility is a bit trickier. How can we train
someone to become more emotionally resilient, flexible,
adaptable, and authentic? To answer this, I again look at
my friends from the military. Young recruits are exposed
to extreme adverse conditions to test their mental forti-
tude, emotional strength, and personal resolve. Do they
have what it takes? They are tested day after day after day.

Some might say this process breaks them down so the
military can build them back up. I've heard it said that the
military removes individuals from their emotional agility to recast them as soldiers who'll follow (or give) orders,
not spend time on independent and creative thinking.
I get that the battlefield is not the ideal spot for brain-
storming and a kumbaya session.

But the veterans I've worked with are agile in their
thinking. They're open-minded, receptive to learning

a new way of being and thinking, and willing to share their hopes, fears, goals, and challenges once they've learned to trust me. Their military training tests their will, emotional aptitudes, and commitment at levels most of us civilians can't imagine. Service members must make quick decisions, often in life-and-death situations, and evaluate all possible outcomes in a split second. Being able to function in such high-stress, emotionally charged environments builds their emotional agility.

Fight, Flight, Freeze, and Fawn Responses

Let's face it: what we're discussing in terms of your ability to have influence is not easy or comfortable. We're talking about going way beyond what you might feel safe sharing and doing, and into territory that earns you the influence you know you're destined to have.

And, for some, the response to the anxiety that such influence can create enacts the fight, flight, freeze, and fawn response. These are very human reactions to high degrees of stress and uncertainty and they show up this way:

- ▸ **Fight:** Taking an aggressive posture toward a perceived threat
- ▸ **Flight:** Running away from a perceived threat
- ▸ **Freeze:** Becoming paralyzed and unable to move in the face of perceived danger
- ▸ **Fawn:** Trying to sweet-talk your way out of a dangerous or threatening situation

We are all human and responses such as these to the idea of sharing your vulnerability—being *agile* and *real*—can feel like danger. *I could lose my job! My spouse! My friends! My followers!* you might think. But being agile means moving past this perceived threat and knowing that you're simply moving closer to your purpose, your mission, and the influence you need to share with others to enlist their support and validation.

Questions to ask yourself:

▸ How can I have more of an agile mindset at work, with my friends, and online?

▸ When I'm faced with adversity or a challenge, do I fight, flight, freeze, or fawn? How can I change this in myself to be more confident in my influence?

▸ Do I flex and adapt to situations around me?

▸ What does agility look like in others when I see it?

Being agile, and having an agile mindset, makes you a learner. You're open to new systems, ideas, people, and ways of doing things that will help you achieve your goals and vision but might be outside your current wheelhouse. Like any set of muscles, agility muscles require practice, repetition, rest, and training for maximum impact.

RULE 8: BE A STORYTELLER to Share Your Why

Once upon a time . . .

Some of the greatest stories start this way. Have you noticed I begin several chapters of this book with stories? A gripping story brings readers in and helps them relate to your message even if they've never experienced what you're describing.

When you were a child, someone—a parent, caregiver, teacher, librarian—likely read to you, leveraging the power of a story to teach a lesson, share a moral, point out an opportunity, or share some history. We use stories for many reasons: to share data, to teach, to convince others of a viewpoint, to demonstrate a lesson or perspective, and to show our humanity.

As I'm writing this chapter, I'm in a hotel in Washington, DC, where I'm delivering a keynote speech at a conference. On the drive to the hotel, my Uber driver and I passed the Washington Monument. I've seen this iconic American landmark many times on previous trips to our nation's capital.

This trip, however, I decided to phone my husband (and family history buff in residence) and ask him about the significance of the monument and how it came to be. He could have sent me links describing the historical significance of the giant obelisk, pointed me to the plaque on which its dedication is inscribed, and encouraged me to remember more of my early history lessons. Instead, he told me a story. He shared how the Washington Monument came to be in honor of President George Washington, how its construction was stopped for a few years because of funding issues, how it's the world's tallest predominantly stone structure, and how millions of locals, tourists, and other visitors have enjoyed its symbolism, grandeur, and magnificence since it was completed in 1884.

My husband loves to tell stories. He regularly takes me through detailed stories of how he grew up, why he chose to go to the premier art school in the US, and how hard he had to work to get in (and stay in) and pay off his education. He tells stories about the first (and the tenth) car he bought, when he held his daughter for the first time, and how he fell in love with me the first time he saw me. His stories are not only heartfelt but also detailed, memorable, and shareable.

I had a boss, years ago, who was also great at storytelling. He was often tasked with introducing new products to the team that we'd then be charged with developing marketing and promotions plans to support. The products themselves were mundane but necessary to the customers we served. It was how my boss told us about the products that made meetings with him like story time at the library—I wanted to bring a stuffed animal, blanket, and juice box to each conversation!

He described in vivid detail how the product came to exist, why it was needed, and the issues it would solve for the people we served, painting pictures in our minds with his stories. By the end of these meetings, I was excited and motivated to do my best to share that story with the media and other stakeholders. His ability to tell a great story empowered others in the room to repeat his stories almost verbatim.

Storytelling Is Both Art and Science

There's a structure and format to a good story—it follows a flow of opening, middle, and end (or close). Some people consider themselves good storytellers, yet the "long and windy road" they take readers and listeners on is exhausting and comes across self-indulgent. I have a colleague like this. At the outset of every story, she inhales deeply and starts, "Well . . ." and I know to buckle in for a ride full of unnecessary, irrelevant rabbit holes before she gets to her point. It's mind numbing and frustrating and seems to happen most often when I'm stressed and on deadline. Some have truly mastered the language, inference, tone, analogy, and cadence of good storytelling. They know how to relate their language to the audience expertly—never speaking over their heads, but helping them feel more informed and intelligent as they learn new information.

Whether you're a content creator, teacher, engineer, or activist, storytelling has a place for you. As a professional speaker, I've been fortunate to share the stage with expert storytellers. I see them draw the audience in with their message, pause at the ideal moment so the audience is bursting with anticipation, and then add the right element of shock, intrigue, joy, revelation, humor, or sadness to create a perfectly timed release of emotion. It's like watching a fabulous magic trick. You don't know what you're seeing until the trick is over, and you realize the ball was under the cup the whole time.

There's a humanness to stories that intuitively comes to some people as born storytellers. These people don't script or craft their stories; the stories flow from them like water. When a situation requires it, the ideal, relatable, and appropriate story punctuates their conversation, tying a bow around the idea perfectly and seamlessly. They share their feelings, ideas, thoughts, and experiences in real and heartfelt ways, empowering the audience to feel the same—whether they've ever had the same experience or can only imagine it.

The art of storytelling is intriguing to me because I see it as where the humanity of vision comes to life. Stories become a unique connective tissue that binds us together as one people no matter our pasts, location, or lifestyle. We can all learn to tell great stories—from the young professional whose new app can change the way we interact to the social activist who never got past high school yet can mobilize a community to end food insecurity; from the college hockey coach who stands in solidarity with her athletes over an injustice on the ice to the marketing manager who offers their views on the company's current position and changes the firm's strategy to be more socially responsible. I've been in the room when these stories are shared, and oftentimes the side that's resisting the idea or vision slowly releases their frustration and rejection as they begin to relate to what's being shared. When these people tell the story of *why* the mission matters, *why* they feel compelled to speak up, and what the world will look like if they remain silent, we're captivated and eager to know how the story ends.

Speak the Language of Your Audience

Telling your story means understanding your people and what they need. Speaking with elevated and sophisticated language can make the audience feel dumb. Speak too simplistically, though, and they could question your competence. A good story must introduce you as an authentic speaker and help the audience feel confident in both your vision and their own understanding.

What if your audience speaks different languages? This often comes up for me as a speaker and author. I've worked in over thirty countries and have learned to be sensitive to stories or examples that are uber American in their nature, value, or relevance. An audience in Asia or Israel or the United Kingdom might not understand or appreciate a story about self-promotion that plays well in the US, for example. This is why *being inclusive* (Rule 5) is critical to *being a storyteller*—remember who you're speaking to and what motivates them.

Similarly, when your audience consists of different gender identities, age groups, abilities, and economic postures, you want to be sure your story resonates. We constantly hear of people who try to relate to a group by sharing a personal story or experience, only to be deemed tone-deaf by members of that group. If you aren't the right person to speak on a topic, consider refraining or, if you must speak, be sure to thoroughly familiarize yourself with the needs, issues, goals, and sensitivities of the group you're speaking to (and consider reviewing Chapter 3).

Use Unapologetic Confidence

A hesitant story, or one that sounds scripted by AI or your marketing department, rarely carries the same impact and value as an authentic one. Your confidence in sharing your story will come through as you express the passion, fear, humor, joy, and other emotions of the story.

Most of us can tell when a computer assistant or scriptwriter is helping shape a message, mostly because it doesn't sound like you: You normally speak in a casual tone, but your story sounds more formal. You are funny and playful, but your story is conservative and distant.

Your story should share your unwavering confidence in the topic, moral of the story, and its desired impact on your audience. Just today, while listening to the response of a celebrity forced to apologize for insensitive comments made to a group she's not part of, my husband looked up from the television and remarked, "Someone wrote some great words for her." I asked how he could be sure she didn't write them. His answer? "I've heard her speak in interviews. She doesn't talk that way." Case in point.

Connect to Your Humanness

Cross-culturally, we tell stories to share the what, why, how, and where of what matters to us. "Once upon a time . . ." sets the stage for the place and time and why the story is worth listening to. While the language, examples, and tone of the story might vary if you're telling it in Japan or India or America or Spain, we must connect the story and the audience to why the issue matters. People who are good at this don't just tell us what we should know—they go beyond explaining the importance of the program, idea, or vision by personalizing the message to say why it should matter to all of us, right now, right here. They sell a vision of what the world will look like by painting a picture with the story, just like the childhood storyteller who spellbinds the children with their fascinating tale.

To do this means tapping into that vulnerable, sometimes terrifying, and raw place at the heart of your mission, then wrapping an appropriate and personal story around it. This allows others to individualize the message and connect to your humanness not as a boss or leader or influencer, but as a real person.

Storytelling Isn't about You

In his best-selling book on business storytelling, *Building a StoryBrand*, author Donald Miller introduced the notion that the hero of a great story isn't you (the company), it's them (the customer). When you consider the stories you tell, ask yourself whether you're more intent on proving your credentials or competence, showing off your successes, and asserting the validity of your opinion, or on demonstrating how your idea will help the person you're talking to. When we make the listener the hero of the story, we show them how the world will be better or safer or happier or fairer because of the idea. We focus less on proving our idea and more on showing how the idea will serve them.

Use the power of storytelling to authentically build trust, advance your vision, enlist your army of supporters, and drive change. Learn to talk about your cause and speak to your audience in ways they'll understand and act upon. Customization works here. One-size-fits-all approaches do not.

A good storyteller is a master at understanding people. They're expert at reading the room, pivoting when the tone and temperature of the audience shifts, and personalizing their message to meet the listeners' needs and goals—and they can feel confident in the recommendation.

Storytelling for you might be:

- ▸ Opening a team meeting or presentation with a personal tale of why the project or discussion is meaningful to you.

- ▸ When explaining complicated data or numbers, shaping the information into a story.

- ▸ Cataloging your favorite stories—ones that shape your vision, clarify your purpose, or illustrate your commitment so you can inject them appropriately into conversations.

- ▸ Finding clever and memorable ways to draw others into your stories, using their names, specific dates, or places, and painting a clear picture of what you're all seeing.

- ▸ When you need to deflect from a challenging topic or discussion, introducing a related but divergent story.

The Greatest Story Ever Told

Do you remember the greatest story you ever heard? Can you recall your parents talking to you about your ancestors? Do you recall what your spouse said to you on the day they proposed marriage? Can you remember when you first learned about God's love?

When my sons were younger, they loved for me to share the story of how they were born. Both had vastly different experiences coming into the world—my older son was born via an emergency induction at thirty weeks. Because I was getting rapidly sicker with something now called HELLP syndrome, doctors weren't sure my son or I would be okay. They insisted on an amniocentesis to evaluate his lung development, which involved a forty-foot needle injected into my abdomen (okay, it wasn't exactly forty feet, but it felt like it!). Everyone was scared, things were moving fast, and the baby was determined to be strong enough to be born. In 1991, premature births were risky at thirty weeks, and they forewarned us that we would not be taking him home; he'd need to spend a few months in the hospital.

Inducing labor is not for the faint of heart. It's grueling and laborious (pun intended). So, when the tall, burly male nurse came in to give me my much-needed pain meds and asked my height and weight, I replied, "6'4" and 350 pounds." He started to write this down before looking up at me and saying, "You are not!"

"Give me as much as if I was!" I barked back.

And with the meds on board, my beautiful little (4.5 pound) premature son was born. He was a fighter. He quickly soared past all the stats and goals the doctors had set for him, and his anticipated months in the hospital turned into days. We brought him home at 11 days old.

My son loves this story because it had all the key ingredients: drama, urgency, humor, levity, love, and warmth. As he grew, my son embodied the traits his mother told him he'd had since birth and carried his resilient and adaptable personality into adulthood.

Stories can do that. They can transport us, humble us, inspire us, and make us cry and laugh—sometimes in the same sentence!

When my clients ask me to describe the outcomes I produce, I try to always frame my response as a story. I tell them a story of a client I worked with who was like them, faced the same challenges or opportunities, and grew into the person they knew they were capable of being, leading others in the process. While I could focus more on my methodology and steps and deliverables, stories paint a much more memorable and experiential picture.

Great stories stay with us. They transcend culture, time, language, and repetition. While many of us will never have a story that lives up to the status of the Bible, we may create important stories that will influence present as well as future generations. What an awesome gift... and burden!

Consider, as you frame the stories around your vision, creating messages that will stand the test of time and will endure as they are relayed by individuals not as well versed in the topic as you are. Think about your stories in advance since most people struggle to come up with a well-balanced and impactful story on the fly. Framing your story in advance allows you to dispense it at will, offering it up like Costco samples, delighting those around you and enticing them to buy the whole box.

When Is a Story Too Personal?

One of the hardest things I had to learn as a public speaker and executive coach was when to share a personal story. After all, my audiences and clients aren't paying money to hear me tell my tales but to teach them or guide them through something. Or so I thought.

I'd wrestle with whether my stories had enough merit or heft to be relevant, whether they could undermine my credibility and competence, and whether my client or audience would see them as too much of "the Lida show."

But the opposite was true. The more I shared my own experience, the more my clients trusted me. Telling a story can show I've been where they are and know how they're feeling, and what worked for me can bond us closer.

But there is a fine line between a relevant and impactful story and TMI (too much information). No one likes a storyteller who does so just to hear themselves talk, work out their problems onstage, or try to garner sympathy. A young sales professional shared a story with me that I initially thought was made up. It simply couldn't have happened. But it did. He'd been part of a large sales meeting where a young female colleague was asked to share her secrets to business success. The topic seemed innocent enough, but when she revealed her key to success, mouths dropped open: she times her important business meetings and conversations around her menstrual cycle. I kid you not! She talked about how she's so in tune with her body that she will change an in-person meeting to a virtual one, refrain from speaking to her executive leadership, and avoid making certain decisions depending on how heavy her flow was.

Say what?

Even in today's inclusive and embracing culture, this level of personal detail is off-putting, uncomfortable, and challenging for everyone involved, not just the male professionals in that meeting who exchanged the clearest, most "WTF?" looks imaginable.

To avoid venturing into TMI territory, think through your stories in advance. Vet them for their relevance, helpfulness, and appropriateness to the situation, audience, and opportunity.

Navigating Powder-Keg Topics

There will be times when your story needs to touch on a pain point, a sore spot, or a hot topic, and doing so will inevitably set some people off. For example, imagine you need to point out misconduct in the company. You've seen the numbers and the track record, and you know what the company is doing is not right (by any business and moral standards). People will surely bristle at this; some may argue, and you could get fired. But you believe it's the right thing to do, and you deploy storytelling to help make your case.

As you frame the story, consider whether an example, testimony, or story from a non-emotional situation or group could make your audience more receptive to the message you need to share. You could share a hypothetical to introduce the idea. This kind of story deflects some of the emotion from the message you'll share and could clearly communicate the reason you're raising the issue, the timeliness of the situation, and the outcomes that could be headed the company's way.

You may find yourself suddenly in a powder-keg discussion when that wasn't your intention. People can misunderstand, not hear you correctly, and form conclusions about your story prematurely. Here, again, *being agile* (Rule 7) is helpful. Stay open-minded to their views, listen with the intent to learn, and respond with confidence. If you can, find a story to help the listener empathize with your situation, understand your intent more clearly, and eventually consider that they may be attacking you without warrant.

This happened to Adam onstage in front of his colleagues, boss, and senior leadership in his company. He tried to tell a story about his recommendation for a new direction for the department. His story landed flat. In fact, some of the references he made weren't clearly understood, his puns were borderline offensive, he left out important information, and his boss's face grew redder with each word that came out of Adam's mouth. In that moment, in front of everyone, Adam pivoted. He didn't apologize for what he'd said, he just took a beat, turned off the projected PowerPoint slide, sat on the stool provided for him onstage, and told a very different story. He spoke from his heart; admitted he was concerned about his vision but believed that with enough input and guidance they could be successful; and showed his influence in real, raw, and informed ways. You could have heard a pin drop in the seconds before his boss started clapping.

Questions to ask yourself:

- When I tell a story, am I framing up my message in advance? Am I clear about who I'm speaking to and what that person needs to know and feel to buy into my vision?

- How will I archive and catalog my appropriate stories so I can retrieve them quickly?

- Am I able to pivot and shift if my story isn't landing right? To influence others, I'll need to be agile and flexible in delivering my vision, and stories can help.

- Can I craft stories that apply to multiple audiences and yet feel specific enough to important scenarios to serve my influence goals?

- Do I share enough of myself to my team, community, and group so they can relate to me?

- Which stories do I have that are off-limits for me to share?

Being a good storyteller doesn't require you to have Hans Christian Andersen–level storytelling skills (if you don't know who that is, look him up; it's worth it!). Worry less about being charismatic, dramatic, and thespianish, and think about being real, inclusive, and confident in your message and how you communicate its value to the audience and situation.

IN A NUTSHELL: Influence flows when we can consistently show people who we truly are, not who we've been taught or managed to be. Our ability to flex, adapt, and still remain true to our values and consistent with who we are builds loyalty and trust with our audiences. And, when we can tell a great story—one that's memorable, engaging, and focused—our influence (story) can be reshared for years and generations to come.

CHAPTER 5

Locate Your *Where*

Where...

Be Visible
to stand out.

Be a Brand
to make lasting
impact.

THE BIG IDEA: To have influence means we see
you. You'll need to be visible to those you serve in
ways that can be trusted, are consistent, and set
the expectation for the experience we'll have being
influenced by you. By leveraging your personal
agency and tapping into your authenticity and
vision, you can drive trusted, enduring, and meaningful impact.

Do you care what people think of you?

I do!

I care that the people I want to serve, collaborate with, or influence know who I am, what I stand for, and how I can make their lives and careers better. When those people know me, know what I can offer, and perceive me as aligned with the legacy I'm building, then I'm creating honest and authentic trust and influence. So, yes, I care what *they* think of me, but not what everyone does.

I remember as a young mother telling my sons, "It doesn't matter what other people think about you. It just matters what's in your heart." And I was half right. Sure, I wanted them to believe in their hearts they were worthy, loved, important, and capable. But as adults we know that how other people see us directly impacts how and whether they'll work with us, align with us, and promote and advance us, or not. Perception directly drives influence.

Being able to influence how someone behaves, thinks, makes decisions, and relates to you has a lot to do with your persuasiveness and ability to drive positive perception. Some of the most influential leaders do not present in a very elegant and composed way, but the impression they make and the way the audience feels is that they're trustworthy. What they have is credibility, confidence, agency, and realness that empowers others to follow them and forgive them when they misstep.

Sharing a vision requires shaping a narrative: it requires the right amount of poise, eloquence, realness, and intrigue to be just spicy enough, but not burn-your-mouth hot. We've certainly seen evidence of this kind of polish in the speeches of political leaders, corporate spokespeople, and even some thespians.

It could be argued that Martin Luther King Jr. was one of the most influential individuals and greatest orators of the last two centuries. He spoke from his heart. His message was clear, and his voice was strong and broke at just the right moment—almost as if he'd scripted it that way (but we knew he hadn't). He spoke to people who needed to hear his message. He made them cry, act, rise, and follow him toward the dream—his dream, our dream. Whether someone watched him live in Washington that day, listened to his speech on the radio (without the benefit of body language cues), or studied him in school years later, his influence is both enduring and compelling.

Your narrative will live in a place and time, along with an audience who'll hear the message. Being able to know when and where to share your message and build your influence is important to ensure the scalability and sustainability of your value to those you'll serve.

Determining Your *Where*

While it could be fun (and exhausting) to be everywhere, it's not practical. No matter how many times you'll cut and paste a message, it isn't the same as being in the right places in the right way with the right people. Determining where you'll share your vision with others is vital to ensuring you're influencing the way you intend.

In-person and online experiences, conversations, and positioning offer differing opportunities and challenges.

Deciding which is best, when is ideal, and where you can leverage your gifts, voice, and confidence can make or break your influence.

Finding and Deploying Agency

To be heard over the noise, to challenge the status quo, to have your argument or point respected, to influence your followers, you'll need to be agentic: to be so confident and assured in your vision that you can stand tall and proud while others doubt. Yes, you'll consider their viewpoints and bring an *inclusive* (Rule 5) mindset, but your confidence in your vision is unwavering and unflappable.

Sometimes your agency (defined as having confidence, assuredness, and authority over one's own decisions and direction) will lead you to influence upward in your organization or community. Perhaps your boss or obvious decision makers aren't the right advocates to support your idea. You may need to identify more remote stakeholders, constituents, and influencers to rally behind your vision.

My client recognized this when we discussed his boss and why he was deemed "successful" in the company. "He has charisma," my client said. A large man, the boss was great at telling jokes and remembering birthdays and had an entertaining, charming personality. But while most of the staff enjoyed his presence, few would go to him with a challenge or idea, they didn't feel he supported them, and they didn't trust him to have their best interests at heart. Charisma and jokes only get us so far, folks.

While there are certain ingredients present in the confident speaker, the charismatic politician, and the authentic social leader, agency is one of the most powerful.

Personal agency is a beautiful blend of accountability, consciousness, confidence, and wholeness that we use to go into the world with our heads held high, our eyes wide and bright, and our hearts curious and welcoming. When we understand who we are, the needs of the people we seek to lead, and how we can deliver an influential message to them, we can (with agency) boldly move forward. A person with agency is attractive (although not necessarily physically so) because we believe we'll be better/smarter/sexier/more empowered by being around them. We feel safe with someone commanding agency. They're trusted, real, warm, and emboldened.

But are they that way naturally? Can agency be developed?

Yes, to both. Some people acquire personal agency without being mindful of it. Their internal filters are so finely tuned they purr like a Ferrari engine. They make good choices, position themselves in ideal situations, and own their behaviors and reactions without hesitation.

Others develop agency as they grow; it gets refined in training programs and through experiences. Coaches, advisors, parents, and mentors might play a role in the curation of this agency.

Deploying agency requires intention. And to share personal agency with others requires a conscious decision to show who you are, to publicly claim your voice and behaviors, and to own your sense of purpose and be the way you are most authentically. This is not easy for most of us.

My own sense of personal agency came through experiences, hard knocks, and generous feedback.

When I started my business, I knew I wanted part of my work to be as a professional speaker. I love presenting a novel idea, helping an audience personalize the message, and seeing the impact and results they achieve when they implement what I've taught. I authentically thrive here!

As I began my speaking career, I was a good tactical speaker. I shared my methodology, crafted appealing PowerPoint slides to reinforce my message, and even sprinkled a few jokes into my programs to offer much-needed relief to my audiences who were chewing on the gristly and important information I was teaching.

And I was a good speaker.

But I wanted to be a great speaker.

I started noticing that when I'd reach the questions-and-answers portion of a program, I'd typically get the same set of questions: "How did you build your personal brand?" or "Why is this meaningful to you, as a business owner?" or "What's been the hardest part of doing this, for you?" What stunned me was that they were asking about me, the person, not my process, research, methodology, or case studies. Me.

So I leaned into that. The next few times I presented on personal branding and reputation management topics, I introduced some personal anecdotes, stories, and examples to support the topic. And these went over with wild success! People nodded, clapped, cheered, and saw themselves in my stories, because they were my stories. Not data. My "where" was clear—my people were in the audience. They were listening and learning and hopeful I could enlighten them into a new or different way of doing things to unleash who they truly are (not who they pretend to be). Onstage, in my books or articles, and in my coaching, my where is when I'm with the people who need what I offer. I find them, they find me, and we grow together.

Being able to let others see you, know you, feel with you, and learn with you is how you can show your humanity and personal agency. Your light shines brightest when you share it with others! Every time I worry that I'm oversharing in a presentation or book, I watch for the reactions of my audiences, and I see that I've barely scratched the surface.

Building Social Capital (Reputation Currency)

When it comes to being online (which, let's face it, we all are), the landscape for showing your agency and influence gets a bit trickier. Yes, you need to be visible, reach your audiences, and impact important conversations, but some parts of you should not be shown online (yes, bikini photos, I'm speaking to you).

Today, it's no surprise that we're spending more time on our electronic devices, frantically typing into tiny keyboards at all hours of the day and night. Studies indicate almost half (46 percent) of Americans admit to spending an average of four to five hours on their smartphones each day. We're connecting with more people, in more places, about more topics than any previous generation, and yet we often feel we have less to say and feel less supported and lonelier.

On social media, our thousands of "friends" are the ones we chronicle and confess our hopes, dreams, fears, and rashes to on a daily basis. They "like" and endorse and share our message with others, growing our belief that we're well loved and validated by people we'll never meet in person. Our online friends share their favorite restaurant/shoe brand/communication technique/tech application, and we buy without considering the cost or impact to our lives, planet, and productivity.

But are we really building influence online? Are we standing tall in what we believe in and advocating boldly for causes and issues we feel passionate about?

This chapter is titled "Locate Your *Where*," so we must include social media. But as with diet plans and underwear, one size does not fit all. In the twenty-first century, social media enables us to build digital social capital that can be exchanged for influence in many circumstances:

▶ The job seeker with twenty thousand LinkedIn followers can tap into that network to do informational interviews, gain insights about career trends, and secure job interviews.

▶ The entrepreneur whose provocative online video statements send viewers to his website can leverage that traffic to grow his email lists.

▶ The celebrity facing criticism can show they're not the characters they've portrayed on television by filming themselves with their loving, wholesome family.

▶ The CEO who's unhappy about a corporate acquisition can sink the company valuation by leaking negative insights about the company to consumers and the media.

Some of the ways you'll trade visibility and digital capital for nondigital benefits aren't ideal or recommended (see the last example above), but some are. When you can leverage a strong, consistent, and focused online positioning strategy to grow your social capital, you can use that followership, and the visibility that comes along with it, to drive attention to important causes, to your vision, and to what you feel most needs attention.

Your Body as Language

If the pandemic did one thing for most people, it stunted our development in social interactions. We forgot how to greet each other (can we shake hands?), behave on an airplane, navigate social constructs in our community, line up at the grocery store, and collaborate IRL (Boomers: that means "in real life"). It's as if being home for nine months turned us all into awkward teenagers at our first school dance. We became unfamiliar with being in the same space as other humans and had to relearn human connectedness.

As if we didn't have enough to worry about, now we must remember to pay attention to the messages we're sending in the things we aren't saying. Our body language is more important today than ever before: communication in how we build influence is much more than the words we choose.

When your head swings from side to side as you're confirming something, if you glance downward as you enthusiastically greet someone (indicating, *No, Chris, I'm not actually happy to be here*), and if you pick at your cuticles like you're digging a hole to China, you're offering more insight into your intention than your choice of words does. Body language tics and motions that counteract our words introduce skepticism and resistance in the minds of our audience. Learn what your "tells" are and then control them so your message can land right.

Think about this: What impression do you get if someone speaks softly and slowly? Personally, I find it annoying. While you might be nervous about your message and that's why you're speaking quietly, your communication style is making me work harder. I must lean in, dial in, and pay attention more carefully than if you spoke at a normal speed and volume.

And, finally, let's pay attention to volume. Sure, if you're speaking to ten thousand conference attendees at the Ball Arena in Denver, Colorado, you'll need to raise your voice a bit. But if we're discussing your project over coffee, I don't need you shouting at me. Take cues from the people you're speaking to and see if your volume is too loud, too quiet, or, in the words of Goldilocks's baby bear, "just right."

As we navigate where to build influence, we must become careful and conscious of the messages our communication (voice, body, and language) sends to others. If your message requires you to stand at the pulpit, get comfortable with projection and gestures (to amplify your words). If your vision requires more careful, select, and individual conversation to build momentum, use intimate and warm communication to your advantage to be sure you're heard.

RULE 9: BE VISIBLE to Stand Out

"I've never really felt seen," she told me. My heart broke. As my client shared her fear of stepping into her power, being visible, and speaking about what she believed in, she related stories of how her narcissistic mother would overshadow her successes, claiming her achievements for her own instead of praising her daughter. "Look what I produced!" her mother boasted to everyone in earshot. Dejected and sad, my client held herself back, always opting for a support role, never lead.

Being seen was a concept this talented, passionate, and skilled woman had never embraced for herself. She believed she would do better to make others look good and take the back seat in situations where her voice and ideas were desperately needed. When company leadership wanted to improve conditions for working women, she neglected to raise her hand and offer her insights, figuring her ideas weren't unique or valuable enough to take the risk. Throughout her career, she had ideas and insights and learnings but kept trying to find someone she could teach those ideas to, who'd take the ball into the end zone and make the touchdown.

She'd married a man who also kept her in his shadow—the place she felt she belonged. Divorce started to free her to do what she was capable of—as her passion and talents peeked out—but she didn't know how to walk, let alone run. The image of the baby giraffe taking its first wobbly and unsure steps was a visual she claimed fully as we talked about her need to find her voice and strength.

As we worked through the steps to help her own her ideas, she started to unfold, literally, in front of me. My message and words were intentionally designed to be inspiring and empowering, and I reassured her I was alongside her at each step. Slowly, her eyes widened, her voice calmed (from a high-pitched nervous chatter to a more composed cadence), and her shoulders visually rolled back into position. "I want this. I need this! But how do I do this and not feel like a fake?" was her first question as the idea started to take hold.

"One foot in front of the other," I assured her. We had a plan—a strategy—and it was a matter of doing step one, then step two, and then step three. Being who she was meant to be (her purpose) took hold. "Oh," she shared, "you're not suggesting I be fake, just that I whistle past the graveyard, as my grandmother used to say." Yes, sometimes we must display confidence before we actually *feel* confident.

"I'm more of a 'behind-the-scenes' kind of guy," another client shared as we discussed whether a promotion to a more visible role would appeal to him. He'd had an amazing career as a corporate public relations professional who wrote powerful speeches others delivered, who pitched other leaders' stories to editors and podcasters, and who enjoyed being backstage for the big events. But his career had stalled, and he knew it was time to start sharing his ideas, his message, and his solutions to global problems. As he wrote his résumé to get the promotion to a leadership role, he realized he'd helped others build things . . . but hadn't built anything himself. "It's time I become known for building the missions, visions, and voices of important people."

The notion of "being visible" can be terrifying. Maybe you came to this part of the book with hesitation, hoping it would just go away or I'd let you off the hook and declare it optional, not mandatory, to building influence. No such luck.

For many people the topic of visibility and self-promotion prompts resistance, eye rolling, and comments like, "If I'm good, the right people will notice." Yeah, not so much anymore. Sorry. The days of punching a timeclock, being on time and on budget, and passively advancing through life are gone.

Today's world—whatever corner of the planet or internet you're on—is crowded, noisy, and filled with information flowing at warp speed. Being quiet, remaining stoic and reserved, and holding your tongue is not how you or your ideas will influence others. And being visible today does not mean becoming a walking neon sign. There are elegant, confident, and loving ways to promote yourself, your values, and your vision such that the right people are drawn to you in the right way to solve the right issues.

Unlike the street vendors I walk past, who madly insist I need to take one of their samples to make my day complete, being visible is not about pestering people and wearing them down to the point where they just take whatever you're handing out. Remember, influence is not about coercion or compliance, it's about a partnership between you and the person you're seeking to influence.

To be a person who can promote and advance a message and mission, you must be out there, in front, leading and seen.

I remember working with a client who was a well-known forensic accountant. He often testified in high-profile, white-collar criminal cases; was quoted in news articles about the latest Ponzi scheme to hit Wall Street; and represented notable global clients. He was quite known, but he wanted to grow his influence within broader communities.

I suggested to him that we could capitalize on the visibility he had already earned and create a strategy to grow his voice in different communities. He shuddered at the idea of being self-promotional. "If I'd wanted to be more vocal," he told me, "I wouldn't have become an accountant."

Does that sound familiar to you? I get that you might have an unpleasant taste in your mouth about the idea of being visible. We often have images of celebrities or Tik-Tokers or that guy in the corner office who purposefully talks loudly when on the phone with clients or his girlfriend. It's obnoxious and off-putting to most of us.

But imagine the opposite for a moment. If you want to influence others with your idea, message, vision, or movement, how can you do so if they can't see you, hear you, and kick the tires, so to speak, of your idea? Being visible gives a face, voice, and context to your idea. We learn to associate your mission or vision with a human being—that person, right there. The tall one with the glasses, curly hair, and all that passion.

Let's take this a step further. If you're seeking to influence your colleagues, do you rely solely on email communication? If you're the boss, do you get up and go over to your employee's desk to give them a message? If you're seeking to drive change for an initiative, are you getting up out of your chair to do something about it (or just yelling at the TV)? When we're visible—on the team, in the company, in the community—we enhance our ability to share our vision, voice, and passion with those around us. It is very hard to lead and influence without being seen.

I wanted to test this rule by asking my followers (more than twenty-eight thousand people) on LinkedIn: How important do you think visibility is to be able to influence others? Overwhelmingly (86 percent), respondents said you must be seen to be able to influence. Sorry to all of you who were hoping you could deploy ChatGPT to build your influence—you need to be seen.

Being visible means using your skills, gifts, and strengths to build up the groundswell of support needed to advance your vision. Social media, communities, your boss (and your boss's boss), and other groups where your influence needs to be felt must know who you are and what you stand for to align and support your vision.

Being visible for you might look like:

▸ Sitting at the conference table instead of in one of the chairs hugging the perimeter of the room

▸ Speaking up when you have insights to share on a topic

▸ Building a more intentional social media presence, complete with keywords and an updated headshot

- ► Offering to deliver the team's ideas to senior management, instead of providing the key talking points to someone else
- ► Presenting messages in person, rather than relying on email, texting, or IM
- ► Raising your hand when the meeting host asks for ideas or questions on a key topic
- ► Volunteering to lead the project instead of relegating yourself to a support role

Visibility Will Amplify Your Value and Values

There's also a difference between being seen (*Yes, Sara, we see you over there waving your hands like you're flagging down a taxi . . .*) and being seen as valuable. It's not just about face time, it's about adding value.

For this reason, self-described introverts can excel here. While an extrovert might find it easier to assert themselves in meetings and have no fear of speaking up or speaking out, an introvert may actually have more influence. When the introvert does speak up and offers valuable content or challenges to the discussion, their rarely used voice can attract more attention than the screaming Type A person over there. I've seen many instances where a quiet and unassuming individual hears the conversation, digests, and considers what's being evaluated, and then—when the time's right—shares their view, recommendation, or objection. The room comes to a complete stop. They've taken the time to consider what's happening, to roll it around in their mouth like a fine wine, and when they speak, others listen.

Introverts have another magic power: many self-help programs have encouraged them to get uncomfortable, speak up, and be part of the narrative. This made introverts great at asking questions, a form of influence that's almost covert and spy-like. The introvert leads the group in discussion by asking thought-provoking and insightful questions; and, while the others do most of the talking, the introvert is credited when the group reaches consensus. Introverts 1, extroverts 0.

This kind of visibility was a challenge for my client, Becky. A manager in a growing technology company, Becky had the skills, certifications, experience, and track record to have not only a seat at the table, but a voice, too. She worked hard, gave 100 percent to all she did, and was well liked by her team and her peers. She was also a self-described introvert. One hundred percent.

Becky's personality and comfort level led her to want to hang back rather than assert herself and be forward. She believed could evaporate into thin air in the groups in which she found herself. Her peers were dynamic and assertive. Her team was confident and vocal. But, even in photos, Becky was always positioned toward the back—and not because of her height.

We did surveys of her peers, managers, and team to assess her reputation and influence in the company. Overwhelmingly, her feedback reflected words like *kind, punctual, helpful,* and *talented.* Not bad, right? Becky wanted visibility. She knew she needed to get uncomfortable to be seen by those who mattered. She needed to hear "valuable, insightful, leader, and influential" to grow her career at the company.

Slowly (so as not to freak her out completely), we used these techniques to raise Becky's visibility. She went into every meeting with an idea, vision, or suggestion for the topic being discussed. She forced herself to insert her idea, vision, or suggestion early in the meeting, to not wait until it had been offered and simply add a passive "I agree," or "I was going to suggest that." She volunteered to lead projects that were visible and important to company leadership instead of playing a supporting role. She respectfully challenged her boss (not publicly) when his reasoning on a direction failed to pass the sniff test.

I remember when Becky shared a photo from a recent on-site team meeting her organization had held. And there she was—front and center, smiling, confident, and visible. She was the same person inside: she was still kind, punctual, helpful, and talented, but she made herself visible. Eighteen months later, she was assigned a lead role in one of the firm's biggest projects.

Your visibility should always align with your authentic voice and style. If it's comfortable for you to speak up, take charge, and be in the lead, ensure you're doing so for the betterment, not the detriment, of the group. If you're more comfortable listening and learning, do so with the intent to offer your voice at the right time, in the right way. But you'll need to be seen to be influencing.

Questions to ask yourself:

▸ Am I withholding my voice because I'm unsure about my value? How can I get more comfortable sharing who I am and what I know to grow my vision?

▸ If others are talking over me, can I assert myself and remain authentic?

▸ When I have an idea or challenge to share, can I take more risk, recognizing that the discomfort of speaking up will only be short-lived?

▸ If I'm not ready to be visible, what will help me get ready? Do I need more information, training, insight, or confidence to be more visible?

▸ What is the real reason I'm resistant to being out there more, to being seen and heard and having my ideas included in the conversation?

Know Your Medium: The Right Place at the Right Time

If your goal is to influence your team, your boss, your board of directors, or some other known audience, you'll identify the places and times that will best get their attention and meet their needs. Stopping your CEO in the hallway outside the bathroom to advance your idea is typically bad timing, but sharing in a private meeting or group setting where the agenda is flexible could be a great opportunity.

As you prepare to sell an idea, know that your target audience has likely already viewed your online profiles and commentary, discussed you and your value to the organization with other people, and watched how you've conducted yourself thus far. Nothing happening today happens in a vacuum. All the touchpoints of influence converge in even the simplest of conversations, and particularly in the most critical. Remember that *consistency* (Rule 6) is vital to building influence.

If your goal is to influence a great number of people, a community or group or country, the medium you choose is also critical. Let's consider some obvious options.

SOCIAL MEDIA

Today, social media and social networking platforms offer tremendous reach for influence. With a single keystroke you can offend, inspire, incite, or motivate others. This reach should be considered carefully, as we've seen social media tools misused to wreak havoc, provoke violence, and share misinformation and untruths.

Social media has positive value in gathering collective ideas; sharing your vision with others who are equally passionate about issues, causes, concerns, and ideas; and motivating people toward change, empowerment, and growth.

Jon is a great example of how this works. Initially, he started his Instagram account with reluctance. He thought it was "for kids" and didn't want to be lumped in with all the influencers who seemed to be peddling products. But for building his profile and visibility (to be known as "outgoing, active, trusted, and a leader in college sports") with his target audience (college-age athletes and their trainers), Instagram checked the boxes.

Jon began posting images of himself working out, running, teaching workshops on avoiding injury, and more. The images were good; the captions were helpful. Then, one day Jon did a video. In the message, he looked right at the camera and spoke to the students and their trainers with heart, passion, knowledge, and resources to guide them to become professional athletes, if they desired. The video was a hit!

Soon, his followership rose as people began waiting for Jon's content and vision. They started looking for him on YouTube (since videos were now his thing), and the followership and engagement on that platform also rose. His audience was interacting with him, asking questions, sharing their experiences, and getting excited about his upcoming lectures, podcasts, articles—whatever Jon was producing, they were buying!

Social media today offers a unique and compelling platform to share your message, build your followership, and engage in meaningful ways. Sure, it's also filled with self-promotion, trolls, and other nonsense, but it's worth having to cut through the noise to reach the people you seek to influence. Always consider the platform, the audience, the cadence of your communications, and the content you'll share. Refer to the Rules to stay focused on building real influence and authentic trust to drive meaningful change, not to gather likes or clicks or followers.

PRINT

Today, it is easy to become an author. Not a good writer? Hire a ghostwriter. Don't have a publisher? Self-publish your book.

The opportunities are endless, but so are the potential challenges. We all know that person who thought their message was compelling and relevant and funny and inspiring, so they wrote a book. Problem is, that the book was garbage, and no one bought it. The result? For

Christmas, everyone gets a book. Instead of a business card, they hand you a book.

Writing a book is an arduous process. This is my seventh book (one, *Reputation 360: Jumpstart Your Career by Building a Positive Personal Brand*, was a complete rewrite of my first book, so I count it as two). When I wrote my first book back in 2011, I clearly recall the excitement I felt handing my manuscript to an editor for a "read." Suddenly, I was back in kindergarten submitting my hand-drawn self-portrait to an adoring teacher, who'd surely confirm my artistic talent! As I'd be self-publishing the book, I hired an editor to read it for contextual flow, substance, logic, and so on.

I was so excited—I presented the manuscript to her like I was about to change her life and she should be excited, too! A week later, she called with her verdict: "It's a great speech," she said.

I corrected her and told her it was a book. "No," she told me, "it doesn't follow the flow and formula of a book."

Hard stop.

After a few deep, painful gulps, I realized she was right: I'd written as I speak—going off on tangents to keep the audience amused and interjecting a joke here and there to keep their attention. Books follow a format. Every book does. If you don't know the structure, you'll have a garage full of your "book" to hand out to anyone passing by.

You can also share influence in other forms of writing—articles, blogs, op-eds—where your message and vision can grow in reach. Consider being a contributing writer to an online publication. (Some of these are paid opportunities where you're asked to submit articles that are then vetted, published, and distributed, and some aren't.) Consider your topic, audience, and writing abilities as you venture out here. Paying to be featured in a leading publication looks awesome on your LinkedIn profile, and sending your published article around to clients and prospects is bananas, but if the article isn't in your area of influence and isn't supporting the vision you're building, then its value is greatly diminished.

In Person: Groups

In-person events, forums, roundtables, speeches, workshops, and presentations are fabulous ways to assert your presence and build your name. Choose the audience, topic, and forum that best supports your message, though. Otherwise, you risk possible overexposure, and without a solid vision or platform, you can be known as "that person I see at a lot of events, but I really don't know who you are and what you stand for."

When you're clear on the message, audience, and outlet, build your influence following the Rules. For example, in the lead-up to publishing this book, I began weaving the New Rules into all my work—my online writing (articles, blogs, guest posts), presentations (onstage, on podcast interviews), videos (my LinkedIn LIVE sessions, YouTube channel videos, and guest appearances on others' channels), and media (print, audio, and video interviews). Doing this reinforces the message that Lida = New Rules of Influence. This is how I'll grow the reach for the topic I'm passionate about and increase the impact of the message.

IN PERSON: INTIMATE

Not to be forgotten are the one-on-one interactions we have with people who are influential themselves, have the potential to be influential, or are at least well known. These people can help us spread the message of our vision and idea because they have the precious commodity of reach—online and in person. An endorsement, shout-out, mention, reference, or referral from someone with a large network of contacts can shortcut an arduous process.

—

The goal here isn't to try to leverage these relationships to "go viral" but to appreciate the vitality of our vision and its potential. Those authentic and candid videos, photos, quotes, or stories have the greatest potential to be spread far and wide, sprinkling their impact like dandelion seeds (although the hope is the resulting plant is far from a pesky garden weed).

Being visible takes some getting used to if you've consciously relegated yourself to the back row. Start small and, as your agency and exposure grow, seek more ways to be seen, heard, and appreciated for the ideas and value you contribute.

RULE 10: BE A BRAND to Make Lasting Impact

To be influential to others—to have your presence and vision understood and adopted—requires a solid and clear personal brand. Your personal brand is how you act, speak, form relationships, and live consistent with your vision. A solid personal brand builds a solid reputation. A weak or inconsequential brand leaves you at risk for misunderstanding, misperception, and being passed over.

Your ability to build, and then consistently promote, your brand empowers you to influence others and to share your purpose, mission, passion, and goals with those who need what you are offering, think like you do, or are resistant but inclined to come around.

Many years ago, I made a statement that's been widely shared: "Everyone has a personal brand, by design or by default." It's true. Whether or not you're strategic and intentional, you are known by others, and the way they know you and feel about you (particularly the people you seek to serve) determines whether or not they'll support you, listen to you, endorse you, and refer you.

Designing and living your personal brand gives you the platform and criteria for leveraging your voice and influence. Through the process of building and promoting your thoughtful personal brand, you can intentionally find and attract opportunities to share your voice, live with integrity, serve others, and build your tribe and impact in meaningful and measurable ways.

If you've already done the work to create and assert a positive personal brand, great. That doesn't mean you can skip ahead. How you maintain and build your visibility and brand will morph and evolve over time as your influence grows, so following the advice here is important.

If you've never heard of personal branding, thought it was just for celebrities and "fancy people," or have no clue where to start, follow these steps:

1. Clarify who you are and what you stand for (see Chapter 2 for more insight). Exploring this might lead you to a value statement or brand tagline. Or not. When you are clear on who you are at the core, at the non-negotiable base, and you've clarified your values (see Rule 3), you can work outward from there.

2. Understand who you want to attract (Chapter 3 will offer guidance here). We talked about service earlier, and who you'll seek to influence and serve is your target audience. The people, communities, groups, and individuals whose perception of you must be on point. They are the ones you care about knowing you for who you are, for what you can offer, for what you stand for. People outside of this group may also learn about you and your value, but your core audience is the one you focus on the most.

3. Identify your desired reputation, also known as your ideal end state. How do you want to be remembered? When you leave a room, a job, your career, or this planet, what difference did you make? What is your legacy with the people you cared about? Clarify this in as much detail as you can, using emotive words (they felt, they experienced, they believed) rather than relying on corporate metrics and data.

4. Consider the reputation you currently own. How do the people who matter perceive you today? In areas where your current and desired reputation don't align, create strategies to bring them closer.

With an understanding of who you are and how you want to be known, you'll actively deploy the tools to showcase your brand authentically and consistently. You'll create a meaningful **narrative** that speaks to your values and service. You'll surround yourself with a **network** of other influencers who can support, endorse, refer, and inform you. You'll build an **online presence** to showcase who you are and what you offer. By curating **content** on topics that support your vision, you'll begin to be aligned with thought leadership. And you'll lean into your **body language, style**, and **presence** to let others know you, see you, and learn from you.

Building your brand might look like:

- Using self-driven filters to ensure you're promoting your values in consistent and relatable ways
- Showing up consistently, letting decision makers see evidence of your value to the organization
- Removing contacts from your online networks when their posts and comments don't represent your values
- Dismissing yourself from unhealthy conversations because you recognize the value of your good name and don't want to risk guilt by association

We see evidence of strong personal brands every day. In all continents and countries and communities, individuals with consistently clear brands show up in business, social justice movements, academia, technology, and nonprofit work. These are the people you feel comfortable being around because you believe that "what you see is what you get" and there won't be any wide swings or great surprises in your interactions.

Think about someone you know. Can you talk about their personal brand, their values, or what you think they want to be known for? Does the experience of being around them feel enlightening, comfortable, intimidating, or overwhelming? Our personal brands set an expectation of an experience and people around you have beliefs about how it would be to work, serve, collaborate, or follow you—is that expectation positive or negative?

Questions to ask yourself:

- What's my personal brand? Have I clearly defined the way I want people to perceive me and expect to feel if they follow me?

- Am I living consistently with my values and beliefs? If not, perhaps that's why people don't trust me or empower me to drive change.

- Do I have a clear sense of where I'm headed? Even if I don't have a picture in mind of what I'm working toward, do I have a direction and sense of purpose and clarity that I'm the right person to fulfill that mission?

- Do I know the right people who'll surround me with love, support, information, and endorsement and who'll challenge me when I need it? If I don't, I may not carry the influence I'm capable of.

▸ What does success look like? When building my personal brand, it's important to have goals and metrics, even small ones. Creating a community of followers online who're also passionate about my cause or vision is one example. Or I might measure the reputation equity I've earned with my colleagues who're now supporting my initiatives and ideas.

Your personal brand is the intentional and focused projection of who you are to the people that matter. When consistently managed, your personal brand becomes trusted, endorsed, and easily referred by others.

IN A NUTSHELL: How you'll share your influence is largely driven by how visible you are and whether you've clearly defined your value proposition and brand to your target audience. We want to serve you, advance you, and help you. Make it easy for us to do so!

CHAPTER 6

Driving Influence

Why...

Be Courageous
and push past fear.

Be Real
and let others see
the true you.

Be Credible
to earn trust.

Who...

Be of Service
to have lasting
impact.

Be Inclusive
of others wherever
and however they
are.

How...

Be Consistent
in who and how
you are.

Be Agile
to learn and grow.

Be a Storyteller
to share your why.

Where...

Be Visible
to stand out.

Be a Brand
to make lasting
impact.

It's one thing to know about influence, it's another to drive it. Going forward, you'll call upon all your realness, strength, confidence, and humanity to move others to action—to inspire them to think differently, be different, and make change.

Now it's time to weave together the Rules.

Lean on your service mindset, inclusive approach, and courage to articulate the issue. Tell others who might not even realize they're being impacted why this problem needs to be solved, and how things can be better. Help your audiences understand the short-term impact to their lives of keeping things as is, and why the timing is right for things to change.

Build on your realness, brand, visibility, storytelling, and credibility to show your personal connection to the cause. Talk about why this issue matters to you and why you're committing your work and resources to creating change. Draw as much personal connection as you can and include your values to showcase why you are the right person to be leading this charge.

Stay *agile* and *consistent* and play the long game. You might encounter a steeper uphill battle than you initially believed. That's okay: stay the course. Remind yourself that agility is a mindset requiring you to be open-minded and flexible, and that you'll have to stand unwavering in your belief. The more consistently you show up and back up what you say (with what you do), the more your message will gain traction.

Here's an example of how this works. Imagine your vision is to create access to a healthy diet for people living with food insecurity in inner-city neighborhoods in Los

Angeles. As a child growing up in East Los Angeles, you remember going to sleep at night, tummy grumbling from hunger, wondering if you'd be able to eat the next day. There was not a lot you could do to provide for yourself (you were a child, after all), and your mother was already working two jobs to secure the little food she could. Your future felt uncertain, scary, and really big.

Now living in Los Angeles, you have served on the boards of directors of several outreach organizations committed to ending poverty and helping correct food deserts in low-income communities. Your work is meaningful and rewarding but doesn't feel like enough.

You've also built a solid career in the entertainment field, working with high-profile studios and studio executives, bringing revenue-generating commercial programming to the networks and to households across the country. Not so fulfilling.

You're now ready to do more with your vision, your professional competencies, and your personal experience. Here's how the formula might look:

1. Lean on your service mindset, inclusive approach, and courage to highlight the issue.

   "Growing up scared and unsure where my next meal would come from, I'm committing to ending food insecurity in my community, Southern California. There are neighborhoods here where opulence surrounds them, but the children go to sleep at night worried about eating. It is my personal mission to serve these children, so the next generation of young people can thrive and be healthy rather than scared.

"I'm nervous about representing these children. It's daunting to be the one who'll be able to help them and shift the tide of their current situation and give them a better future. But I know that children of all ethnicities, religions, and backgrounds deserve to have access to healthy and nutritious food."

2. Build on your realness, brand, visibility, storytelling, and credibility to help sell your personal connection to the cause.

"I remember the first night I was keenly aware that we didn't have food in the house. I'd woken around 2 a.m., tummy making all sorts of loud noises, and went to ask my mother for something to eat. With pools of tears in her eyes, she told me, 'Not right now. We don't have anything. I'll try to find food tomorrow. I promise. Try to drink more water.'

"I was hungry. I would eat paper or anything to make the pain in my stomach stop. It was summer, so there wasn't even the option of getting food from the school programs. I wasn't sure when I'd eat again.

"This memory haunts me. I am a talented entertainment executive with a thriving career, but I'm also that little girl who was hungry more often than she wasn't. I'm taking my message to our local politicians. I'm leveraging my network—including the nonprofits I've served with—to do something about this. We'll be launching an initiative called Kids Eat in LA, and I'm asking for your funding and support.

"I value service. I've learned to help others and be of service to people who need me. I'm also competitive. You can hold me accountable to fulfill this mission. Watch me, join me, or get out of my way. This IS happening! With my vision, no child in Los Angeles will go to sleep hungry again."

3. Stay agile and consistent to play the long game.

"I've developed a two-year plan to make this initiative a reality. Honestly, we don't have much more time than that. If we can't take care of these kids and make sure they're healthy and thriving, we'll lose a generation of Angelinos. We can't afford that.

"These kids are your future college students, your employees, your entrepreneurs and bosses and writers and politicians. We need them healthy.

"I'm open to your ideas. While I have the vision and the plan, we need to work together to make this real. I will be holding town hall meetings regularly, and I'll be visiting your companies and election headquarters and shareholder meetings to ensure everyone knows about this mission.

"Did I mention I'm competitive? I go after what I want. And I want kids in low-income neighborhoods to have food *security*."

Humans Crave Humans

Remember, humans crave social connectedness. We strive to be aligned with others who move us toward our personal greatness. Sometimes that looks like following people online who're championing beliefs we also hold.

Sometimes we show up in person at events where we know no one. Sometimes we resist the temptation to sit by ourselves at lunch and join a table of strangers instead. We're social creatures and need to be around people who'll support us, grow us, and motivate us to think and be who we're supposed to be.

At work, our need for social connectedness is why we're pushing back on endless meetings and email discussions. We want to hear and see and feel the presence of those we work with. Research is indicating that video meetings won't disappear, but their use is changing. No longer are we just idly sitting back watching someone talk "at" us on camera. Today, we require interaction, participation, and collaboration. Tools like virtual whiteboards and in-meeting voting systems and other collaboration tools are putting us on notice: audiences want to be involved in the conversation, and not just as bystanders.

Influencers

Today, we call people "online influencers" because they've amassed (or bought) large followings. They boast about their 5 million "followers" to indicate people want to be led (and influenced) by them.

Influencers tend to fall into two camps: the ones who promote, sell, affiliate-market, and push brands and products to their followers; and the ones who share a message so compelling and influential to their community that their followers flock to them. Consider Tim Tebow, a sometimes-polarizing sports figure. Tebow's popularity often had more to do with his consistent and unwavering commitment to his faith, acts of service, and millions of followers than to his passing yards on the football field.

And then there's the Kardashian-type influencers. While I applaud their ability to leverage notoriety to grow businesses, employ people, and offer products people want, they appear to lack a commitment to most, if not all, of the New Rules of Influence to grow a meaningful legacy.

People who use their platform to provide inclusive, helpful, supportive, and compelling messages reach their followers in relevant, personal, and meaningful ways. They let us see their realness—their vulnerability—and they are confident in how and where they'll show up and lead. Yes, they've built a brand that's consistent and clear (sometimes with the help of PR and branding teams), and they leverage this brand to grow their influence and impact on others. Many do so to shift a narrative, grow their voice, and lift or help those who don't have the reach they possess.

Influence works when someone we trust, like, envy, fear, or respect endorses or stands for something. Because we feel a connection to the individual, we also want to like or buy or avoid what they say they're liking, buying, or avoiding.

This is not a new concept. When I was in consumer product marketing, we routinely sought out celebrity endorsers or spokespeople who had wide appeal to represent our product. The people who liked the celebrity would then like our lipstick or camera. It's no surprise, then, that online influencers have sprung up as a viable career field with seven-figure incomes.

In business, influencers look a bit different. They might have corporate cachet and a Midas touch for products or initiatives that are "no fail" to budget decision makers. While you and I might need to present our case by amassing supporting data, running scenarios to show low risk, and presenting a well-organized pitch to senior management, these corporate influencers simply smile favorably at an idea, and it's blessed by the powers that be.

How did they gain such favor? How do they possess the ability to exude presence and confidence and surety in complicated arrangements? The answer: they weren't born this way; they spent time earning and building trust, honing a meaningful and clear personal brand, and being visible to the right people in the right way.

Influence Hacking

There are no shortcuts to being influential. Remember, influence isn't the same thing as notoriety. You can be notorious for bringing an assault rifle to an airport. Having influence means following the New Rules—much harder to do and more impactful.

As you work the Rules and embody the vision that you'll passionately and confidently communicate and use to drive change, start:

- ▶ **Raising your hand.** Sure, someone else may offer that same idea, but why not take the chance that your idea is more fleshed out? Take the risk and be courageous and bold with your advocacy of your mission and vision. You may be wrong and need to regroup, but maybe not. Influencers are willing to take the chance.

▶ **Being prepared.** In day-to-day interactions, think ahead to what could be important and relevant. Then, come to meetings and interactions ready with an idea to share. If someone else shares the idea first, build on it. You'll have thought this through in advance and can show how strategic a thinker you are.

▶ **Becoming an expert.** You won't carry long-term influence if you're a short-term thinker. Become well versed in your area. Whether your goal is to become an online influencer helping women feel better about their bodies or to motivate a community to hire better teachers, you'll need to know your subject. Learn, research, listen. Then, when you offer your idea or insight, others will hear the subject matter expertise.

▶ **Using silence strategically.** Having influence doesn't mean always speaking up. Learn to offer silence in ways that show your agency and thoughtfulness. Sometimes the loudest voice in the room isn't the smartest one. A silent pause in a conversation, speech, or collaboration will always feel longer to you—you've created the pause. Others will likely take note, reflect on what you've just said, and consider their feelings and approach while you give them the space to do so.

▶ **Demonstrating inclusivity.** Rather than saying you embrace inclusivity, show it. On social media, be sensitive to the feelings of people who may have a different experience than you do. In presentations where you'll show slides or offer examples, be sure to represent diversity to show your inclusivity.

- **Listening.** When you're doing the talking, you're not listening. How can you be learning? Practice holding back at times, letting others speak, and then contributing a point that's not been considered. This might sound contradictory to my "be sure to voice your views" message, but it's not. It's about balance. If you're the only one talking, then others can feel talked at. But if you take time to consider and reflect on others' points of view, you show inclusivity and you may learn another viewpoint.

Stop:

- **Interrupting.** No one likes to be cut off mid-sentence or mid-thought. It feels dismissive and rude and likely makes the interrupted person reluctant to contribute again. Yes, you're excited to share your idea, thought, belief, point, opinion, or data, but so are others. Pace yourself in conversations to find a cadence of they speak, I speak, they speak, I speak.

- **Apologizing.** Ugh. I still do this one. Sorry for sharing an idea. Sorry for walking through the door before you. Sorry for existing. . . . Unnecessary apologizing diminishes our credibility and can create the perception of eroded confidence. Yes, we should apologize if we cut someone off in line or interrupt them without warrant or hit them with our suitcase as we retrieve it from the overhead compartment on the airplane. But apologizing for sharing and being? No. Let's make a pact that we'll get rid of this nasty and useless habit. Are you with me?

▶ **Tilting your head.** Women, we do this a lot! When delivering hard or important news, when sharing our views or standing in our confidence, we tend to tilt our head instead of keeping it straight up. To us, this might feel warmer or softer, but to the person seeing this, it signals insecurity and submissiveness—neither of which are good for influence-building. Keep your head high and share your vision!

▶ **Hesitating.** There's a distinct difference between strategic silence and hesitating. When you pause, you're letting someone else get a word in. Used correctly, strategic silence builds rapport and relationship, as others feel part of the conversation. Hesitating is where your nerves take over and you freeze. You start questioning your validity and worth and whether you'd best remain silent. Online and in person, hesitating can cost you the opportunity to make a difference, to be the leader we need, to serve in the way you need to.

Traversing the Challenges of Having Influence

Having influence, and being influential, isn't always unicorns and rainbows. There are times when it's difficult and frustrating and more doors close in front of you than open. There are times when your message is met with resistance or lack of enthusiasm, and you may question your commitment. There are times when your vision brings up old garbage and issues from your past you'd rather leave buried in the backyard, where they belong. Let's look at how to deal with those here.

Battling the Naysayers

How will you influence people who aren't on board and don't support your vision but are necessary to your success?

For example, if your plan is to drop out of grad school to start a nonprofit that brings integrated technology to small villages in remote parts of Africa, it may be important to have the support of your parents, who might be shell-shocked by their investments in your education without the return they expect (a shiny diploma!). How will you convince them of your passion, commitment, and confidence in your idea and maintain the relationship?

Or, if you're trying to influence your boss, the board of directors, an investor, or the media that you're worth taking a chance on for a vision you see for the future of the team and organization, how will you navigate through their objections and resistance?

It's easier to build influence when everyone around you is singing from the same hymn book. It's when we need to be convincing, endure the resistance, and continue to push through with our resolve that we often find the most benefit.

We'll always have people who challenge us, play devil's advocate, and oppose just for the fun of it. My father was one of those types. A brilliant man, he never met a vision or idea or even a suggestion he didn't initially rip apart to see what the guts looked like. A frustrating experience when I'm a ten-year-old sharing my vision of what I want to be when I grow up: a zookeeper!

When you can remain open, agile, real, and considerate, these naysayers will reveal if and how they need to be convinced. Don't take the challenges as a refusal of your complete vision and idea; it just might need some refining and tweaking. Listen to their objections and see if they're valid. The more open and curious you are to learn, the more clear and confident in your rebuttals (incorporating their concerns and questions), the more you'll be able to adapt and scale your message to others. You'll learn to accept that other people will share those challenging ideas and want to see you show tenacity in your vision. This is a good practice and muscle to strengthen.

(By the way, when my father pointed out that being a zookeeper didn't mean I'd get to play with the animals, ride the giraffes, and cuddle the koalas but rather had to manage the staff, make tough decisions about the animals' health, and balance a budget, the shine came off that fantasy.)

Leading Others through Turbulent Waters

In addition to dealing with naysayers who may question your ideas, there will be times when you'll be called upon to lead and leverage influence during tough times. Conflict resolution pros will tell you that deploying tools such as capitulation, compromise, coexistence, and collaboration (lots of Cs!) is necessary. So is your ability to navigate influence.

When do you go out front? When do you hang back? When is your voice loudest, and when do you let others share the ideas first?

Change and uncertainty are difficult for most people, and how you navigate turbulent waters with others watching and looking to you for safety and assurance is the stuff leadership training courses are made of. For us, let's look at how influence helps here:

- You may not have all the information or direction you need to positively influence those around you. In those situations, rely on the Rules of *being courageous* (#1), *real* (#2), and *inclusive* (#5) to identify the right moves—what to do first and next. You may need to listen more than you speak, show your vulnerabilities to encourage others to do the same, and share concerns before they become issues. And you may need to be so self-assured that you don't question yourself anymore. Project yourself as a leader, and don't waver in the face of adversity.

- Your *agility* (#7) and *credibility* (#3) will require you to stand for your values and behave accordingly, to pivot and flex when needed to reach the goal. You'll not compromise your values, but you can create greater community with others when you show a mindset of agility and openness.

- Knowing that change is uncomfortable and stressful, leverage your *consistency* (#6) and *brand* (#10) to authentically build trust in what you say. When the people around you believe you're there to *serve them*

(#4) and are being authentic, they can trust that what you share is the truth as you know it.

▶ Get out in front of the issue rather than waiting until someone approaches you. Remember the importance of being *visible* (#9) and resist hiding from important conversations, but rather lean in and leverage your *courage* (#1) to navigate the unpleasantries of a difficult situation.

▶ Deploy your *storytelling* (#8) skills to rally the troops and engage others with you, even if you lack all the answers at the time. Ensure your story is relevant, applicable, and empathetic to the situation at hand, and put yourself into the story not as the hero but as a part of the equation.

It's often hardest to build influence during the hardest times, but that's also when our influence matters the most. Make the choice to raise your hand, offer your insights, protect and help others, and build your community regardless of how easy it feels in the moment. Remember, I've got you—and you've got this!

Losing Influence

What if you've been a person of influence—online, in person, at work, in your community—and then you lose it? This is indeed a tricky one!

There are several reasons why we can lose influence. Perhaps you break someone's trust by acting in conflict with your professed values (as discussed in Chapter 2). Restoring trust and credibility takes concerted time, effort, and patience. And you still might not earn their loyalty again. Going back to the fundamentals and articulating who you are, what you care about, and who you seek to serve (and influence) is a big step toward regaining trust.

Online, you might recommend a product, person, service, or company that later falls out of favor with your community. This often happens when someone backs a person and promotes them to their followers, only to find out that person has a sordid past or makes a poor decision. Now you need to earn back the influence of those followers who believed in you and supported you. Explain the error in judgment, show how you'll be more careful next time, and then take steps to be more watchful going forward.

Balancing Influence with Authority

Influence, like trust, is a precious commodity. Be careful how you use it, and never abuse it. When someone believes in you, follows what you recommend, and supports your vision, you've acquired a very special relationship. Cherish and protect it at all costs.

As you build your influence, it's normal to feel a new sense of authority in the world. Now, when you speak, others listen and act. You bring agency and credibility into conversations, whereas in the past perhaps you were hesitant. You feel the authentic trust you've built and curated with the people you seek to influence and lead.

It's hard for all that influence not to go to your head.

But I'm asking you—imploring you, actually—to resist feeling authoritative. You've earned the right to have influence, to be influential, and to make a difference and drive change. When ego and authority and entitlement enter the picture, the glass cracks. Influence is like trust; it's earned and must be maintained. Too much self-focus or posturing can fracture influence, and before you know it, you're back at the starting blocks. Do not pass Go. Do not collect $200.

Surround yourself with people who'll hold you in check and keep you accountable to your vision. Empower them to push you out of your comfort zone, let your truest self and voice shine bright, and grab you by the suspenders and pull you back into line if you head into danger. Lean on them, love them, and trust them to have your best interest in driving the impact you're capable of.

Your choice to drive influence; to be a person whose words, vision, and actions matter; who may change the world, or a conversation, or a project is exciting! Embrace the challenge you've chosen to take on. Know you're not alone—there are many of us out here doing exactly the same thing. We're confident and bold (and sometimes scared), because we've thought this through, and doing what we believe we were designed to do is our only option. Our passion and commitment to what we know is possible, who we seek to serve, and where we're headed is non-negotiable. Please join us!

Conclusion

Measuring and
Living Your Impact

Have you heard of the *Tetris* effect? I was introduced to the idea by a colleague. Research into the *Tetris* effect notes how long-time gamers (particularly of the popular piece-sorting game *Tetris*) begin to recognize patterns in everyday life—say, how boxes are stacked at the grocery store, or how suitcases can be stored in overhead bins on the airplane—because of the sorting techniques and skills they developed playing the game.

Other researchers have studied this phenomenon to note how someone can make connections or correlations between seemingly disconnected things that somehow the subject sees as a recognized pattern.

Why am I talking about gaming and patterns here? Because influence works that way. You'll want to measure your impact on those around you to gauge your effectiveness, but there will be a pass-along value to your voice that's much harder to see, touch, and claim. You may be training someone to see the world more inclusively and to develop a servant's heart, but when they end up using that new skill outside of your view, it could be hard for you to see. For this reason, you'll need to trust and believe that if you've followed the Rules laid out here, your impact will grow in far-reaching ripples.

Influence metrics range from key performance indicators (KPIs) to online engagement, word of mouth, and gut sense. You'll want to reflect on how others behave and respond to your vision, but some of your influence and impact will come through intangible qualities and more subtle shifts.

So, how do you know if your efforts have been successful? How can you tell if you've truly influenced your people, or if they're just going along with you? How will you measure your influence? Did you achieve what you set out to do? Let's unpack that here.

Measuring Influence

You may need to simply "trust the process," and know there's impact to your vision. Not every influential person gets the gold star or trophy at the end of a speech or project. Look for signs beyond the obvious checkmarks or pats on the back to say you've done a good job and others are following you. You'll need to look for people considering what you've said or asking clarifying questions to show they're trying to digest the idea. Look for people who'll commit to baby steps toward the direction you're promoting. Those are very good signs of your impact.

Practical ways to measure influence can include:

▶ **Engagement metrics.** If you'll be promoting your influence online, for example, you can see metrics around the number of comments and shares of your content, and how many people are supporting your message with "likes" or "loves." This can give you an idea of how well your vision and message are resonating, especially if you dig deeper and look at who is responding this way. If it's your core target audience, that's a good sign.

▶ **Feedback.** In-person, written, or verbal surveys and feedback tools can help you understand if your message is on target and relevant to the people you're seeking to influence. Companies do this all the time. Ask for input on how well others understand your goals, voice, and vision, and whether they align with the mission or cause. Pay attention to who gives you the feedback and what they are saying.

▶ **KPIs.** Key performance indicators related to your message, intent, goals, or reach can be helpful to assess how effective your efforts are. For example, if you've relied on word of mouth to grow participation for a cause-related event and people aren't registering, perhaps deploying social media tools would help. Then, you could measure results from both and see which is more effective in getting your message out to the right audience to drive participation.

▶ **Collaborations.** Your goal might be to leverage the reach and influence established by others (influencers in your area, not only on social media). This can substantially extend your message. Always assess the quality of the partnerships and collaborations you enter. Just because someone has access to the right audience doesn't mean their message, values, and vision align with your own. Combining multiple collaboration methods can help you scale your vision, particularly if time is important. When you believe your vision and mission to be better or more meaningful than a competitor's, getting to market first can be crucial.

The Intangible Benefits of Influence

Some of the more qualitative ways of measuring your influence and impact will come in the anecdotal comments your audience shares with you: the tears in their eyes when you share your story, how they grab their pens and write down your call to action, and when they tell others about you and your work (especially when you didn't specifically ask them to).

You'll want to pay attention to your own internal compass as you take more risks (being courageous), show more realness, flex into your agility, bring more voices into hard conversations, refine your understanding of who you serve, and consistently and credibly show up as you (your brand) out in front, where you belong. Ask yourself:

- ► Am I excited to get up each day and sell my vision?
- ► Do I see myself inspiring others?
- ► Am I energized by my voice and stories?

- ► Who's inspiring me?

- ► Am I drawn to new conversations and communities—how can I serve there?

- ► When I feel most confident, what am I doing and who am I with?

Finding Inspiration

I promised myself (and my family) that I wouldn't turn this book into a woo-woo diatribe of motivational sayings, group hugs, and gratuitous affirmations. That said, there's an important idea to introduce here.

Those of us called to influence others on a grand scale—whether it's in business, politics, social change, healthcare, environmental sustainability, tech, or interplanetary space exploration—need to be inspired ourselves.

So, who inspires you? Where do you draw your creative energy? This simple question points to your influence lifeblood. If you said you're inspired by Gandhi, then read all his works; study his life, his followers, and his impact. If you're inspired by your disabled child, then spend time watching them, marveling at how they approach life's challenges and opportunities. If you draw inspiration and energy from reading the Bible or the Torah or the Gita, then move it into a daily practice.

Implementing the New Rules of Influence is hard work, and you'll need to stay inspired. You'll need to draw creative juices from the world around you to keep focused on the mission at hand. Otherwise, the naysayers, challengers, and effort can become overwhelming, and you can lose momentum or focus.

There are times in my business when my "paying work" takes over my focus and I find it easy to displace my commitment to help military veterans through their transition. My military-focused pro bono coaching calls, speeches, workshops, and in-person events feel like distractions from what keeps the lights on for my business. I must sometimes remind myself that not only am I performing acts of service to people who are grateful and generous and have served so I can live in a free country, but I also get inspiration from them. Their stories, challenges, and passion inspire me to want to do more, be more, and share more.

Consider enlisting an inspiration partner whose role is to keep your coffers full, keep you motivated, and keep you focused on the goal of serving and saving and helping and leading as you're designed to do. At work, this might be a colleague or your boss. You can share your ideas about your vision and plans and let them know that this will be personally challenging for you, given your background, your workload, or the company culture. You're 100 percent committed to making things better and need their help.

In your community, you might ask a few like-minded leaders, who are also passionate about creating change or advocating for the same cause, to support you through the times when it feels easier or more acceptable to look the other way. Again, spell out what you need from them—go past basic metrics, and lean in to inspiration, energy, and deeply felt passion. Can you do that?

Finding Influence

Look around your office, organization, community, industry, country—who is influencing you? It may be the new hire who demonstrates a warm and welcoming approach to helping the team grow. It may be your executive director, who rolls up his sleeves, along with his team, to serve in the community. It may be a politician who's willing to share the hard truth about where the community is headed under current policies. It could be the young woman who says "no more" to how she and other women are treated under cultural rules.

The good news is that anyone of any background can aspire to a place at the table to share their voice. The old rules of sitting on your hands for a decade before you've "earned" the right (and the look and the training) to speak up are over. The bad news is that the New Rules of Influence haven't been clear until now. We've heard that purpose, passion, and authenticity outweigh old factors like dress or status, but for many people, balancing these can feel like walking a tightrope.

Get Out of Your Own Way

Writing this book, at times I've felt like I'm declaring a call to arms—for you to rise up; own your narrative, purpose, and vision; and charge forward, no holds barred. And perhaps that's the point. Maybe the goal in writing and reading a book like this is that we need to be inspired and pushed and supported; we need authentic leaders who'll influence from their hearts; and we need to find them (you) wherever they are in the world, in businesses, communities, and countries we can't find on the map.

If you're a young person with a passion to speak your mind growing up in today's complicated, exciting, and curious times, I have a message specifically for you. Many of you strive to be different, unique, and special to feel your most authentic. You promote and assert your style and views and taste and individuality on social media, in corporate settings, and in coffee shops around the world. Your creativity, talents, and ideas are innovative, courageous, and mind-blowing, and the world desperately needs to hear from you!

At the same time, because of how human nature works, without realizing it you may be introducing artificial barriers between you and the people you want to influence, especially if they're not like you. You may be trying to promote your ideas to corporate executives who are more focused on your nose piercings than the validity of your vision. You might decide that protesting is how you make your voice louder, rather than speaking calmly to a politician who feels as passionately as you do about a topic and could be convinced to make change. And you might believe that to be authentic and individual means it's up to others to change and adapt to you, not the other way around.

Perhaps you're right. Perhaps one day the world will look past the visual cues you're sending and the words you're using to express yourself and get to the heart of your issue more quickly. But I believe you can embrace your realness and still navigate the barriers unnecessarily inserted into conversations. There is tremendous value in personal expression—especially since it often comes from cultural, ethnic, spiritual, or private beliefs and norms. But if the audience you seek to influence, who needs to understand and value you, is distracted and resistant to the experience of you, is that serving your ultimate purpose?

I'm not suggesting you fully code switch and cover the tattoos, abandon your identity, and don a red power tie. Heavens, no! Instead, understand how perception works and use it in your favor. People will judge what they see, hear, and experience. Express your personal convictions, showcase your individual beliefs, and under no circumstances erase yourself. Just remember there's another person across the table from you who might find the message—tied up with the purple hair, torn jeans, and metal spike through your eyebrow—a lot to digest. The work and the dream you have to share is worth some small accommodations (maybe slick down the hair to modify the mohawk, wear a t-shirt without a political slogan, and remove said eyebrow spike) to build community and connect with others who will believe in you and your vision.

Can You Buy Influence?

Years ago, I was approached by a talented professional—a leader in his field by all accounts. He held a position of authority such that what he said would be executed without much questioning, and his visibility in professional and social circles made his face recognizable at the grocery store.

When we first met, we talked about his goals. "I want to be influential," he proudly uttered. I asked him what that meant. "I want to be famous, to be invited to highly visible stages, maybe do a TED Talk (not a TEDx), write a best-selling book, and amass a large online following." He then went on to say he was in the process of making that happen: he had hired a ghostwriter to write his book, planned an expensive splash marketing campaign to drive attention to the publication, and intended to preorder enough copies to secure its spot on the *New York Times* and Amazon Best Sellers lists. He'd hired a publicist to book him television and podcast interviews and write bylined articles for him. He was in the process of searching for a personal branding specialist who could refine his image and land him on the red dot (the TED stage).

With trepidation, I decided to help him bring his voice to the masses. I truly believed there was an authentic person under all this fluff and fame-chasing, and I was committed to bringing that forward. I believed, at the time, that with all his expertise and exposure and track record, if we could showcase who he was as a person, we could amplify his influence and truly make a difference to people who'd benefit from him.

When I presented my recommended strategy to him, his response floored me: "Who can I hire to execute all this?" I reminded him that he must bring this to life. It's his voice, his passion, his vision that needs to tell the stories, show inclusivity, be brave, and be vulnerable. He couldn't just hire someone to create a mask that he puts on when he needs to.

And that's when we parted ways. While he'd sold me on the belief that he truly wanted to be a thought leader who shared his insights to influence and inspire others, he wasn't willing to follow several of the Rules (particularly numbers 2, 3, and 5) needed to be relatable, inclusive, of service, influential, and trusted.

Yes, I've worked with clients who admit they bought online followers, incentivized their teams to align with their vision, and otherwise coerced their followers into action. The perceived influence they attained is not, in fact, "influence" but mere cooperation.

Influence Is All Around Us

Look at influence in other mediums, like art or music. Not just the Beethovens or Dalis or Monets. But the Banksys, the Kawses, the Swifts, and the Oliver Anthonys (a mostly unknown singer who released a country song in 2023 about the rich people in Richmond, Virginia, and sparked a nationwide dialog about the impact of wealth on the middle and lower class in the U.S).

I look at the influence of African artist Kehinde Wiley, whose work I was fortunate to experience in Barcelona's Museum of Contemporary Art (MOCA), where I learned about his story. He made it his mission, his purpose, to challenge the limiting way traditional Western art had represented images of power and Black identity. His art showcases the power, grit, tenacity, and beauty of the Black community in a complex yet loving social and political environment. He's said, "Art is about changing what we see in our everyday lives and representing it in such a way that gives us hope." In this way, he's using his voice to change a narrative and influence a culture.

We Need You

Your people need you. Your team needs you and the world needs you. I need you. We need to see you and hear you and listen to what you have to say.

Sure, it will feel scary, maybe downright terrifying! But so was the first time you rode a bike or asked someone to marry you or left a cushy job because your moral compass couldn't fake it anymore. Influence is about galvanizing around an idea. It can be a small one or a large one. Articulate what's needed to drive that impact, then put yourself in the visible, confident, and scary position of leading that impact. This is how we authentically build trust and drive change. The world isn't changed for the better because we fear fear. The world is made better because we stare fear straight in the eye and go forward, right at it. You'll succeed not *because* you were afraid, but *despite* being afraid.

Begin:

▶ **Taking chances.** The reason change hasn't happened could be because the universe has been waiting on you to come forward. Being courageous means asking yourself, "Is it me?" who should lead that charge, offer a great idea, or point out that the emperor is butt-ass naked instead of waiting for others to go first and then adding a limp, "yeah, I was thinking that, too." Be bold, be courageous, be the *you* the world has been waiting for!

▸ **Asking questions.** Just because something has always been that way or done this way doesn't mean the time isn't ideal to change those tides. Challenge the status quo. Throw a flag on the play and ask for a time out to consider alternative paths forward. Bring the smartest and most resilient, underrepresented, and experienced person into a room and ask them questions. Your inquisitiveness could be the secret sauce to finding more opportunity and joy and potential going forward.

▸ **Leaning on others.** Let people around you who love you and believe in you help you succeed. Take their comfort and advice and wrap it around you like Grandma's favorite blanket. It's your new suit of armor and it will help you get through the inevitable challenges you'll face.

▸ **Taking accountability.** Own your mistakes along with your successes. When you apologize, show empathy, validation, and commitment to human connectedness.

Influence, as you've seen here, is a choice, not a state of being. You're not born into influence, you don't get handed influence with a new business card or promotion, and you can choose not to have influence if you reject it.

When you choose to have influence, to be a person of influence, you'll know that authentically building trust and enacting the change you want to see in the world are how you'll deliver on your promise of your purpose for being here.

I've spent most of my career helping companies and leaders advance a message, promote an idea, and further a cause. I've worked to build a platform to help individuals around the world create and project their personal brands. The goal for these people was to be seen, heard, and known for who they truly are and what they truly offer.

I realize now that what they seek *more* than competitive advantage, status, redemption, visibility, or money is influence. To know that their vision, message, voice, and life matter. To understand the reason they're here right now and know they'll be recognized for who they truly are and appreciated for all they truly offer. They want influence. Don't we all?

Acknowledgments

A book like this is possible only with unwavering love, support, guidance, and endless cups of coffee provided by the people who believe in me and this topic.

To my clients and colleagues who've honored me with their realness, thank you for trusting me to tell your story so others may benefit from your experience. You are the example for what we aspire to, and I appreciate you.

To my fabulous publisher, editor, and the entire team at Berrett-Koehler—thank you for encouraging me to speak my truth and share my vision, and for being such a collaborative and empowering partner in this journey to reframe a powerful narrative. Neal, you pushed me way outside of my comfort zone, and I'm so glad you did!

To my team at LIDA360—Sabrina and Kristen—thank you for holding down the fort as I buried myself in this content. I couldn't do it without you! And a special thanks (again!) to my adviser on this book, Kathe. Once again, you've been an invaluable sounding board as this book took shape.

And to my husband, Scott, who gives me more courage, forgiveness, patience, and love than one person deserves. Thank you for always being my biggest cheerleader. I'm a woman blessed with a remarkable family (Beau and Cris, Clark and Grace . . . and the littles!) and my dear friend Eileen, all of whom let me brainstorm themes and ideas and hold me accountable to share my story in ways that will serve others. I love you all!

Index

About the Author

LIDA CITROËN (@LIDA360) helps global executives, entrepreneurs, and thought leaders manage how they're perceived and drive them toward ideal opportunities. As a personal branding and reputation management authority, she empowers individuals around the world to position themselves for influence and success.

Before starting her company, Lida spent twenty years in corporate marketing, PR, and business development, leading global product and services companies across multiple industries. In 2008, she formed LIDA360, LLC, and built a reputation as an award-winning author and executive coach, in-demand keynote speaker, workshop facilitator, and go-to source for media interviews.

Lida's popular TEDx Talk, her Talks at Google presentation, and her numerous courses on LinkedIn Learning showcase her empowering coaching style and message. She is also a faculty member for the Institute for Management Studies, presenting seminars throughout the United States. Lida routinely teaches in-depth and actionable programs on personal branding, digital (online) positioning, influence building, reputation management and risk, and leadership.

A writer for Entrepreneur.com, Military.com, and SWAAY.com, Lida has authored countless articles and is featured in international media including *Time* magazine, MSNBC, *Fortune* magazine, Forbes, Inc., Entrepreneur.com, Military.com, *Harvard Business Review*, Bloomberg, Kiplinger's Personal Finance, *US News & World Report*, HR News, *US Weekly*, Investment News, Money Watch, HuffPost, Monster.com, and more.

Lida has authored numerous award-winning books, including:

Control the Narrative: The Executive's Guide to Building, Pivoting, and Repairing Your Reputation

Success after Service: How to Take Control of Your Job Search and Career after Military Duty

Reputation 360: Jumpstart Your Career by Building a Positive Personal Brand

Your Next Mission: A Personal Branding Guide for the Military-to-Civilian Transition

*Engaging with Veteran Talent: A Quick and Practical
Guide to Hiring, Onboarding, and Developing Veteran
Employees*

A passionate supporter of the military community, Lida volunteers her time to help veterans transitioning to civilian careers. She works closely with employers who seek to hire military talent and serves on the board of directors for Project Sanctuary, a nonprofit committed to healing military families. Lida's work with veterans comes from gratitude for their service and sacrifice.

Dear reader,

Thank you for picking up this book and welcome to the worldwide BK community! You're joining a special group of people who have come together to create positive change in their lives, organizations, and communities.

What's BK all about?

Our mission is to connect people and ideas to create a world that works for all.

Why? Our communities, organizations, and lives get bogged down by old paradigms of self-interest, exclusion, hierarchy, and privilege. But we believe that can change. That's why we seek the leading experts on these challenges—and share their actionable ideas with you.

A welcome gift

To help you get started, we'd like to offer you a **free copy** of one of our bestselling ebooks:

www.bkconnection.com/welcome

When you claim your **free ebook**, you'll also be subscribed to our blog.

Our freshest insights

Access the best new tools and ideas for leaders at all levels on our blog at ideas.bkconnection.com.

Sincerely,

Your friends at Berrett-Koehler